PENNIES TO
THOUSANDS

BUILDING AN ABUNDANT TRADING ZONE

TRADING ZONE—A AREA YOU CREATE AROUND YOURSELF WITH THE INTENSITY OF A POSITIVE FEELINGS.

THE TRADING ZONE IS NOT JUST YOUR PHYSICAL AREAS IT'S YOUR WHOLE BRAIN AND AND ENERGY ZONE.

PENNIES TO THOUSANDS

DR. MICHAEL KLUZINSKI

PENNIES TO THOUSANDS

iUniverse books may be ordered through booksellers or by contacting:

iUniverse
1663 Liberty Drive
Bloomington, IN 47403
www.iuniverse.com
1-800-Authors (1-800-288-4677)

ISBN: 978-1-4917-8618-5 (sc)
ISBN: 978-1-4917-8619-2 (e)

Print information available on the last page.

iUniverse rev. date: 12/22/2016

CONTENTS

Risk Disclaimer... vii

Foreword xiii

Author's Preface xvii

Introduction.. xix

How to get the most out of this book?.................................. xxxi

1   Trading Psychology...1

2   Fibonacci numbers 35

3   Low Cost Stocks Under $8 40

4   Candlestick Signals 55

5   Magic Indicators 62

6   Types of Orders..82

7   Money Management 85

8   Putting it all together 90

Appendix... 101

Acknowledgments.. 121

Risk Disclaimer

Although every precaution has been taken in the preparation of this book, the publisher and author assume no liability for errors and omissions. Furthermore, neither the author nor publisher are liable for any damages, either directly or indirectly arising from the use and the misuse of this book. Use of this book hold harmless the publisher and author.

The publisher, staff, agents, representatives, affiliates, subsidiaries, successors and assignees, are not liable for any claims, losses, cause of actions, loss profits, loss opportunities, indirect, special incidents, consequences, punitive or other actions and including, without limitation, court cause and alternative fees.

Losses against the actions resulting from or imposed upon the use of any of the publications are designed to provide accurate and authorized information regarded to the subject amount covered, it is so at the understanding that the author and the publisher are not engaged in rendering legal account or other professional services. This disclaimer also applies to any social media or any websites associated with the author and publisher. If legal advice or any expert systems are required we recommend the services of a competent licensed professional.

There is a very high degree of risk involved in trading Low Price stocks. Past results are not indicative of future returns. Dr. Michael

Kluzinski and all individuals affiliated with this ebook assume no responsibilities for personal trading and investing results. The indicators, strategies, columns, articles are for educational purposes only. Traders results are individualized and can't be applied to any general measure.

Your use of the trading observations is entirely at your own risk and it is your sole responsibility to evaluate the accuracy, completeness and usefulness of the information. You must assess the risk of any trade with your broker and make your own independent decisions regarding any securities mentioned herein.

This risk disclaimer also applies to all web pages, social media, blogs, videos or audios; associated with all subjects of PENNIES TO THOUSANDS, TRADING HAPPY BUDDHA and GLOBAL TRADEXX INTERNATIONAL S. A.

Dr. Kluzinski and employees are not licensed by any government agencies. The information in this book is for educational purposes only. Please check with your tax financial advisor or broker if you have any tax questions.

*Dedicated to my readers who are going
to be my future trading gurus...*

Which one are you?

There are many people that, after reading the title of this book, will be curious but also skeptical and will fall in one of four groups.

The first group are the disbelievers. They simply refuse to believe that any system can turn a small amount of money into a large amount. Maybe no amount of evidence nor website can convince them.

The second group are skeptical. They don't believe that the system works but if they get enough evidence they will start to consider it.

The third group are what I like to call, "The Cautious Believers." These people believe that they can turn their small amount into large amount but they don't believe any claim they read; they demand evidential proof, they demand examples of everything.

The fourth group are, "The Strong Believers." This group believes anything they read or hear and it makes sense to them. This is a pretty good group because they take and use their ideas and ultimately become richer faster. But don't worry, all groups can win. I am hoping that as you become a strong believer you will post your stories on our Facebook page and help the skeptics of the world become richer. Also, I hope you become a member of our trading community on our "Pennies to Thousands" website. This site will have a traders chat room, audios and videos.

WHENEVER YOU ARE ON THE COUCH WATCHING TV NEWS OR LISTENING TO THE RADIO NEWS DO YOU FEEL TERRIBLE AFTERWARDS? LET ME EXPLAIN 24 HOUR NEWS, TODAY GREETS YOU WITH MASS SHOOTING, CATASTROPHIC NATURAL DISASTERS, OR SOME CRAZY POLITICAL CANDIDATES. SOME NEWS IS MARKET RELATED MOST IS NOT.

TURN OFF THE TV OR SWITCH THE CHANNEL AND
TUNE IN TO YOUR INNER MIND WHEEL OF FORTUNE.
GUARD YOUR TRADER ZONE AREA.
THE BLUEPRINT IS HERE.
YOUR DREAM LIFE IS A CHANNEL AWAY.

FOREWORD

This book is going to turbo charge your trading. Pennies to Thousands. It's a wholistic brain trading approach to change your life. In this book you'll go over details, step by step instructions on how to trade effectively, which also includes philosophical techniques that will teach you how to use the left side of your brain and how to use positive statements and visualization on the right side of the brain.

We're going to leverage the left brain-right brain connection to lock in your profits in trading. It will give good profits within your control. We will use the premiere techniques of harnessing your mind's power to improve your trading in both the left and right brain to shape your life and move toward your dreams with your trading profits. I GET IT AND I CAN HELP.

Here we'll teach you how to reach your trading goals, how to clear your negative beliefs, visualize and affirm, and anchor your positive trading goals with exciting visualization, combined with the ancient power of Fibonacci Numbers, Candlestick Signals and Magic Indicators. Remember it all starts with your imagination. Imagination is the ability to see yourself using this system and having a new and improved self-image. The stronger emotions and more people you include in your imaginations will increase your progress.the more joyful emotions you bring in to the process the better.

Your goals in this book will include trading goals and what you want to do with your extra money as a result of your trading profits.

The technique goes something like this: you imagine the desired outcome in your mind, you DEC the negatives (We are going to explain that later but it means Delete, Erase, Clear) and at the same time after the negatives you repeat a positive statement in the present tense with your visualization anchoring with something physical, like touching your head or slapping your fingers with your mind joyful. Remember no matter how happy your end goal is, the most important part is to start feeling happy and positive no matter where you are starting from. This is because the energy you are using to get to your end goal will get jump started by matching the happy energy you start with. To find joy look for things to be grateful for.

There are strong scientific evidences that this type of system can dramatically improve your results. Some of the greatest thinkers of the world — Einstein, Edison, Jung, Tesla and Carnegie — all believe in the power of the mind to influence activities. We are going to use these concepts with our magic indicators to help you develop your intuition and right brain systems in order to have an excellent trading style. IT'S CRUCIAL TO MAKE POSITIVE LASTING CHANGES. NEW RECENT STUDIES HAVE SHOWN THAT OUR SUBCONSCIOUS MIND, THE INNER MIND IS MILLION TIMES MORE POWERFUL THEN OUR CONSCIOUS MIND.

Norman Vincent Peal was quoted as saying, "Live your life and forget your age." I believe that 100%. But what do you believe? I've been referred to as the Buddha of happy trading, which is a philosophy that will be expounded upon more throughout this book. I'm telling you Pennies to Thousands can be done by a 21 year old or an 89 year old. If you can sit in front of a computer and your eyes are still good enough to see the screen with or without glasses and you can still hit key strokes on a computer keyboard, you can reach your trading goals. It doesn't matter how old you are. Sam Walton got started at 44 years old in Walmart. Charles Darwin wrote the origin of species at 50. Colonel Sanders found Kentucky Fried Kitchen at 65. It doesn't matter the age. You can reach your trading goals.

The baby boomers are aging and they're starting to retire. They were spenders and now they're becoming savers. Many of these savings are coming in retirement plans like IRAs, SEP IRAs, 401 K programs, etc. The next generation has problems with endless debt and large student loans. This system can help this generation to reduce their debt and reach their goals.

Everyone's goals vary. Everyone has things they want to do and accomplish. They want to contribute to their community, give to their grandchildren, provide extra for their children. Maybe they want to open up a business, profit or non-profit. This book will help them to do it.

I DO NOT LIKE FIXED INSTRUMENT PRODUCTS BECAUSE INTEREST RATES HAVE BEEN LOW FOR TOO LONG THEY WILL GO UP AND THESE THINGS WILL THEN GO DOWN.

"Gentlemen who prefer bonds do not know what their missing."

-Peter Lynch.

Benjamin Franklin wrote: *"Do you value your life?"* The value of anything that you obtain, accomplish or experience can be determined by how much of your time, physical and mental, you spend to acquire it. The amount of your mental self that you use to achieve your trading goals, whether it be part time or full time, is an important factor to consider before you begin. Only by discovering your innate mental strengths, developing and exploiting our trading system can you achieve the satisfaction level you want from trading. Decide what you want to have and do, place your mental and physical resources, and just like a famous sneakers company once said in its logo, "Just Do It".

Before you get started ask yourself 5 questions:

1. What do I most enjoy about trading?
2. How would I describe my ideal trading day?
3. If I want a large amount of money trading stocks how would I use that money?
4. What are my unique talents and abilities about trading?
5. Accent your strengths and DEC all your weakness

Are you ready to eliminate self-sabotage, fear and uncertainty and start actively pursuing the dream trader's life that will give you the confidence you crave to be a good trader? I've got good news for you. You're in the right place and I'll show you the right materials. BRING AS MUCH JOY TO THE PROCESS THAT YOU CAN. WE ARE GOING TO FOLLOW THE MONEY FLOW.

Good Luck on your trading journey!

AUTHOR'S PREFACE

People always ask me: *"If you can trade well why do you want to teach?"*

I enjoy teaching. I love helping my students. In fact, I get a good psychic income for helping other people trading the market. I also enjoy the social aspect of teaching. Trading can be a lonely business. That's why I recommend you to get in a trading community. I also enjoy helping others reach their goals. I love to look at my emails and seeing my student's results and helping them overcome their financial obstacles. I like helping students reach their goals. That's what this book is dedicated to. I help others become successful traders because I find that when you help your trading community you help yourself.

MY JOY IS THE SATISFACTION I GET FROM HEARING GREAT RESULTS. I BELIEVE THE KNOWLEDGE I GIVE IS ALIVE. KNOWLEDGE IS THE POLLEN OF THE TRADERS UNIVERSE. SOMEONE MUST ACT AS A CARRIER TO MOVE THE POLLEN. WHEN THE POLLEN STICKS, THE KNOWLEDGE TAKES ROOT AND GERMINATES—GREAT TRADERS ARE BORN.

INTRODUCTION

Benjamin Franklin, the wise man, reminded us that a penny saved is a penny earned. This has become the symbol for wealth and prosperity and in this book we're going to teach you how you can turn those pennies to thousands by using the principles in this book. We're hoping you discover an unfair advantage over all other traders.

How would you like to earn an extra $425.00 a day or $100,000 a year and be able to do anything you want with your family, doing in it in very little time with very little effort and making everyone proud and erase the smirk off your brother-in-law's face?

Why does the market feel like something's off? Why can't we use a buy and hold strategy? What feels so wrong?

CNBC (a financial station in the United States) doesn't have answers and major investors are wondering what's going on. Why is it so hard to make profits these days? Why am I so frustrated with my trading and its reinvesting results?

Well, I'm going to make this as simple as it can be. The market today is different than it was before; before we had to pay close attention to interest rates, we still have to pay attention but a lot less because the movement of interest rates are very small. Today, our FEDERAL RESERVE JUST PRINTS MORE AND MORE MONEY.

The Europeans and the Japanese are doing the same thing too. And you're wondering, what kind of stock market trading strategies can I use here?

They say that eighty percent of all the buying you watch today is run by the Big Boy's institutional investors. Even a large CBS news program announced it. ITS TOUGH IN THIS MARKET. GOOD CHANCE YOU FEEL STUCK,TRAPPED ANS FED UP.

Now, who is included in this eighty percent? They're not the little guys. They're the big boys. They're the whales. They're the mutual funds. Even big companies have large amounts of cash balances that are getting into the game. So that means that eighty percent of the stock market, trillions of dollars, is ran by a very few elite.

Who is after these people then? That leaves you and me. The trader and the investors. They like to call us the "market peons". In this book you will learn the way the institution trades. How can I buy low price stocks that the big boys don't get into before the whales get in?

You'll say, *"Well, fundamental analysis."* I'll tell you fundamental analysis is somewhat a waste of time. Sometimes before earnings it is helpful. This is something I do look at but very little. But stock price behavior, which is the key, is really unpredictable. It's mysterious.

I'm telling you there is always news out there. Governments are going to shut down. Let's face it. Out there today it is kind of like trading on Star Wars. Do you trust any fundamentals? I wouldn't. Are you trusting the old technical styles? I wouldn't. The buy and hold? I don't. So getting ahead is hard, getting ahead is tough. That is why I'm writing this book.

WHY DO SOME PEOPLE SUCCEED IN THE MARKET WHILE OTHERS FAIL? THE MARKET IS THE SAME. SO WHAT'S THE DRAMATIC DIFFERENCE IN RESULTS? THE

INNER MIND YOUR TRADER ZONE, IS YOUR REAL SECRET COMPONENT IN TRADING AND INVESTING.

Can you go back to the old ways? I don't think so. You see that in the world today the middle class is being squeezed but these hedge fund people keep spending money. They bought a mansion that was worth close to a hundred and fifty million dollars. Guess who bought it? A fund manager. Two fund managers just purchased a professional NBA team. The highest price ever paid for art was purchased by another hedge fund.

Did you hear the story about these top institution managers that decided to give a party and they took a private jet around the world for a whole year? Even the top fund managers out there are throwing extravagant holiday parties. Sometimes they send their guests the invitations engraved in gold!

But this is the tip of the iceberg. The wealth is becoming more concentrated on the institutional side of things and the old ways don't work. The ways I'm going to tell you will teach you how to be nimble and how to keep learning.

To look at the new Magic Indicators you have your subconscious working for you to get rid of all the negative attitudes and beliefs. Old beliefs won't help you trading at the section of the market where the big boys aren't concentrating. Your subconscious mind determines your real success in trading long term.

The single worst mistake you can make is to pretend -THAT THINGS STAY THE SAME- The hopes of independent little traders getting blown up, accounts getting swallowed up… and then people going to other methods like buy and hold, but that won't work either. You might say, "I'm going to collect my dividend cheques." Well, dividend cheques aren't that much anymore.

A lot of you are feeling stuck. A lot of you have to get unstuck. That's why we first present this book dealing with your subconscious to get rid of your negative attitudes and beliefs. Then, we tell you to work with your magical indicators, candlesticks and money management. And then what? Then we tell you a section of the market to look at, the under-eight-dollars ones and some special magical indicators to work with. So don't worry up to this point, it's not your fault. Reality has been fighting against you and this book brings you good news. I'll tell you how to adapt.

You could start with a small account size; you don't need five thousand dollars. You'll be able to sleep like a baby because of these built-in protections and you won't have to be glued to a screen all day. You can go out with your buddies or go to have lunch with your grand-children or whatever you want to do. The complete system is here, I wish you the best. I wish you to become the *guru*. I BRING THE BLUEPRINT YOU THE JOY AND EFFORT.

- - -

In today's world, about every 8 minutes, people lose their attention span and for this we have very important points to help shake those cob webs loose. I'll try to keep things moving in this book but about every 21minutes get up and stretch, do whatever it takes and bring your attention back. Today's market is different.

So let's look at the facts:

Fact #1: The price of oil plunges and spikes. UNDER 40 DOLLARS A BARELL.

Fact #2: Currencies are quickly moving against each other.

Fact #3: Interest rates are at a low CD and money market rates are abysmal.

Yield is hard to chase today. The more you want, the more junk you have to get and that's risky. The doomsayers have always affirmed "the world is going to crash". Well, they keep bringing more money and the effect of that is the market is going higher. We need to pay attention to what it is, not what we want it to be and we have to understand this printing of money since cash needs to find a home so we can trade the markets correctly.

The market is a different place. It moves faster. The old technical indicators don't work. In fact, when I started in the late 1970's there were times where you could get high interest rates on treasury bills and get double digit returns, but those days are gone.

A lot of people ask me, *"How much time is it going to take for me to do your DEC program? How much time everyday is it going to take?"* Well, it can contain as little as 3 minutes in the morning, which is a Fibonacci number, and 3 minutes in the evening. That's as little as 3 minutes to make your program, to open your subconscious minds and receive the correct trading matrix that you want. By doing that, it is so powerful that it's going to reprogram your mind; take away the negative and let in the positive if you think you can take that. Remember, the stronger your emotions are linked to your goals and intentions, the quicker the results.

We can't use the 2005 mentality to handle a 2016 market. We always have to look for an edge. Where is our edge in the current market philosophy of today? That's what this book and my website will help you with and the other *gurus* have decided that if we put more indicators this might be the answer. FEEL THE JOY OF A LOW PRICED STOCK GOING VERTICAL

In reality, we have to find the best indicators, the simplest indicators and what we really need to do is to price action. Most people don't like to look at price action because they like some other way to confirm it. But sometimes, price action with simple indicators is the best way to go.

I'm always going through the list of over 200 indicators to find the best that fits. In today's market, we have to rethink the problems and details, not how we would like the market to act because the market does exactly what it wants to do. Do you ever notice that the best ideas really come from nature? We tend to over complicate the situation. The best solutions are out there. That's why I use the Fibonacci numbers.

- - -

Markets are like living beings: they work just like us; they run as far and as fast as they can in their initial excitement and passion but then they get exhausted. Then they go sideways or downward until they recover. After that, at some further point, the trend changes and that's just like how we climb a mountain: we don't go straight to the top, we might go to one base camp, let our body adjust and then we go to the next base camp, we let it adjust and so on...

There are millions of people buying and selling things in the markets. We have to think like living beings, like nature.

I've got my favorite indicators: (that you're going to learn in this book) price action with candlesticks with certain indicators that will help us measure the organism called the market: a living breathing thing. I HAVE THE FORMULA. YOU THE POSITIVE FEELINGS.

We are always looking for the edge and that's why it's very important for us to clear up any negative beliefs out of our subconscious; allow the subconscious to attract to us as many solutions as we can in that area. That's why we have to learn how to anticipate, not just react.

It's like talking about tennis, we have to anticipate where the ball is going to be for the player to move. In today's market, you always have to be anticipating where the next price is going to be. You've got to be in it to win it. You have to anticipate the next move and be like the tennis player who is asking, *"Where is the ball going next?"*

You're in the best place to hit it. Most traders today are looking in the wrong place, using wrong tools that maybe worked twenty or thirty years ago but they're not working in this QE driving market.

Sometimes, the major trend is one way but then the minor trend can reverse and it always reverses from the inside out. First, you'll have an inner day time frame — like 21-minute time frame — that will start the move followed by the daily and then weekly.

Imagine you've been trapped. You've been trapped in a cell trading like in jail trading. Sometimes you make money, sometimes you don't. Sometimes you lose big, sometimes you win small. Sometimes you physiologically beat yourself up, sometimes you just make the wrong moves. So one day a psychiatrist comes and you hire him to come to the jail cell with you. He says, "Boy, you are not trading good. This is not a good place for you in here." He is smoking his pipe and you are asking yourself, "Why are the psychiatrists always smoking pipes?" Your second thought is, "I want to get out of this jail cell and you are telling me it's not good for me. BIG DEAL!"

I come along one day and I come into your trading jail cell and I'm not going to make any comments in how your trading jail sets up. I just say, "Here is the key. Get out of here. There are better places to trade. There are better states of mind to trade, there are better ways of trading, better rules and better discipline." At the end which is going to be more effective? The psychiatrist, smoking a pipe, making comments of where you are: in a jail cell, or the person that gives you the key to get out to find a new way, a new hope and a new system? PAST MISTAKES BELONG THERE,CLEAR NEGATIVES, LEARN LESSONS BRING ON THE GOOD STUFF.

- - -

Many people ask me what platform to set up. I would like to suggest a newcomer to the field.

They actually have a fundamental research company that is called ZAC's trade. They have lower cost, a powerful platform (which I think is important), international trading price and trading exclusion. They also have exclusive fundamental research which I don't really get into much in this book but it's good to know about it. Their commissions are about half of the big boys and they have affordable trading programs.

"Risk comes from not knowing what you are doing"

-Warren Buffett

In fact, they have a trading program called ZAC's trade PRO which really has a lot of features and a lot of trading stations. They can even diversify if you want to do some international trading.

They dynamically, every time, every second, are re-routing to win, getting the best price and there are fast changing market conditions, so they'll give you a legend in that area.

Then, the final edge. The BIG EDGE is the HUGE one. It helps you get a free subscription to this ZAC's premium from ZAC's investment research. ZAC's is a good fundamental (not technical) place to start.

It is also good to have some fundamentals, for example: maybe you have two stocks that have the same indicators. Well, maybe the difference could be fundamental research. Choose a good trading platform you like the best that has trading sessions and where you get the best executions. Always pick the strongest stocks in the strongest groups, and also where you're getting the best commissions. They are a big thing and you should feel comfortable with that. ANY TRADING PLATFORM IF IT FITS YOUR NEEDS FOR SPEED, PRIVE AND EXECUTION.

The ZAC's platform is a new comer to the game but they are not a new comer to research. They are huge with fundamental research in the investment business and that will be a good player in the trading platform business. You can find them on ZAC's trade or zacs.com, they have a toll free number (188889792257) and if you have an account somewhere else and you switch it over in an efficient transfer and they will actually give you some cash back.

So there are many advantages to it: you trade what you want — once again, where you are the most comfortable with. If you're looking for a suggestion many people send me emails, call me or ask me. I'm telling you that is one of the places I recommend. They even have mobile platform. For example: if you want to trade from your phone, tablet or any other electronic device; you don't necessarily have to be tied down to a desk. They have a good mobile trading platform.

If you want to borrow money they have low margin rates there too, but I recommend you not borrow money. If you are not trading much they don't have any inactive fees and they don't have any trading minimum so they can measure commissions. ZAC's trade really is one of the best in the industry leaders.

I did some independent research done by a 3rd party. They determined that the ZAC's trade price executions where significantly better than the industries.

YOU NEED EXECUTION SPEED AND A GOOD INTERNET CONNECTION.

I WOULD SUGGEST A GOOD TRADING COMPUTER WITH SPEED AND GOOD MEMORY I WOULD PROVIDE SO FOOD FOR THOUGHT IF YOU DO NOT HAVE ONE, CALL EDDIE AT EZ TRADING COMPUTERS 800-387-5250, ASK ROR THE SPECIAL PRICE FOR TRADING HAPPY BUDDHA. OR http://eztradingcomputers.net

- - -

BUY ANY GOOD TRADING PLATFORM THAT WILL WORK FOR YOU.

I started my career in trading and got my first job after I graduated from the University of Delaware in 1976. My first trading job was with Merrill Lynch, in Baltimore, MD. In this job I learned the importance of doing your own research and using technical analysis to make a trading decision.BETWEEN FIRMS I DEVELOPED A COMPANY CALLED INNER MIND DYNAMICS WHERE I STUDIED THE WORKINGS OF THE INNER MIND. MY FINDINGS ARE HERE AND ALONG WITH YOUR OWN MIND YOUR GOALS WILL BE MET. I AM THE MAN IN THE EARLY 80'S WITH INNER MIND TECHNIQUES AND SUBLIMINAL TAPES THAT WERE SO SUCCESSFUL. THIS UNIQUE BACKGROUND OF A PHD IN FINANCE ALONG WITH INNER MIND TECHNOLOGY LEADS THE WHOLE BRAIN EXPERIENCE. IN THOSE DAYS

I WAS AHEAD OF MY TIME AND CONSIDERED A LITTLE WEIRD. If I could I would send all of you a personal email or a telephone call to encourage you to do your own research.

- - -

I am not a hero. I just have over 40 years of trading experience. I have made all of the mistakes and I'm here to help to prevent you from making the same mistakes. I am going to teach you through our trading community that I'm not the hero but you are the hero by using our shared beliefs and telling stories on our Facebook page, websites and other social media. Our trading community that includes videos, audios and comments from our subscribers will help you understand our systems. THE REAL KEY IS EVERYBODY TRYING TO HELP TO KEEP THE ATMOSPHERE PLAYFUL, JOYFUL AND POSITIVE.

I am just human like you, a common man that has decided to teach my daughter, who is in ninth grade, to learn the proper way of trading. She is helping me write this book to remind me that we must keep everything simple and easy to understand for the unexperienced. I need to mentor you and help you get unstuck from your negative ways of trading. YOU NEED TO KEEP YOUR MIND PLAYFUL AND JOYFUL.

Please post your successful stories on our Facebook page and other social media to help the others in the trading community. I am reminded by my daughter to be humble in writing this book, so I won't tell about my personal triumphs. I will rather let my trading community tell their hero stories and fulfillment of their desires and overcoming their road blocks on all aspects of our social media (Pennies into Thousands). PLAYFUL NATURE WILL HELP YOU AND OTHERS REACH YOUR GOALS FASTER.

How to Get the Most Out of This Book?

As you read this book you will be exposed to multiple strategies that have a high probability of success but not 100% guaranteed. This book has a unique chapter on how to clear negative attitudes and negative beliefs from your trading mind. For this reason alone the book is valuable to all traders. In my years of experience, I have found that all traders no matter what their experience have some sort of negative experience that has affected their subconscious mind and trading, some have very little others a lot. Most books don't even address this subject, but I feel this is a large bonus in this book. WHATEVER SYSTEM YOU TRADE YOU CAN USE THESE INNER MIND SYSTEMS TO BECOME BETTER.

My book is different. It has new current ideas that dispelled the myths about trading and misconceptions about trading. The ideas from this book and our trading community, along with the website, will help you reach your goals. FOCUS ON WHAT YOU WANT CORRECTLY AND WATCH IT BEGIN MANIFESTING.

Remember, the big boys have high frequency trading that have their high speed computers linked to the exchange computers. So, in trading, we have an us vs. them mentality. If you trade 20 days a month and you make as little as $425.00 a day you will make an extra $100,000 a year; the big boys use automation and trading tools in real time, thus, we have to learn to automate and have a trading community that can use the website to get information. This system will work for the newbie trader and parts of this book will help the veteran trader. Learn to paper trade or use small amounts of money first before actually put in your hard earned money. Some of the things you will learn in this book are:

- How to stay in control of your emotions when you trade.
- How to unblock your negative attitudes.
- How to create a winning subconscious trading strategy.
- How to use buy/stop or sell stop orders to protect your trading capital.
- How to use trading scans to get your best candidates for trading.
- How to find excellent candidates for low price stock selection.
- How to increase the return in your retirement accounts so you can have a dream retirement when you decide to retire.
- One secret moving average to help you stay longer in the stock.
- Why you need to develop an us vs. them trading mentality and you have to learn to find the advantage
- How to find and maintain an edge.
- How old edges do not work anymore.
- How to recognize and adapt to new markets as they come.
- And much more…

OUR WEB SITE WILL CONTAIN SHORT 3 MINUTE
UPDATED AND CURRENT INFO TO HELP YOU
STAY IN YOUR TRADING ZONE. FOR NOW
SOME TIPS- THINGS TRADERS DO NOT DO
DO NOT JUDGE OTHERS

DO NOT CRITICIZE OTHERS
DO NOT GOSSIP
DO NOT CONDEM
DO NOT LOOK DOWN ON OTHERS
DO NOT SPEND LIKE THERE IS NO TOMORROW
DO NOT BE COCKY
DO NOT BE OVER ASSERTIVE
DO NOT RELY TOO MUCH IN OTHERS
DO NOT HURT OTHERS
DO NOT LOSE YOUR TEMPERS

KEEP HAVING WONDERFUL TRADING DAYS

—LOA TZU-*"THE JOURNEY OF A THOUSAND MILES BEGINS WITH ONE STEP"*

1

TRADING PSYCHOLOGY

"THE SIMPLER IT IS, THE BETTER I LIKE IT"—PETER LYNCH

FIRST SECTION IS WORTH THE PRICE OF THE BOOK ALONE.

Traders are very individual people; they are lonely people, they have to feel a strong worth and value. Traders need positive self-esteem. Your subconscious mind holds the key to your self-esteem. You can trade your mind with our DEC (delete, erase and clear) and affirmation systems used in the alpha state. Discover a revolutionary trading strategy that is so powerful that it helps transform your trading mind from a consistent loser into a super good trader, faster than anything that existed before.

There are so many expensive *gurus* that tell you about the systems. Have you ever asked the *gurus, "How are your student accounts going?"* I'm concerned about how well my student accounts do.

To be a successful trader you need five things:

1. Trading system with a platform.
2. Risk management and money management.
3. A proper state of mind of trading.
4. A good internet and backup internet system.
5. You must eliminate all negative beliefs and become part of a trading community. YOU MUST CHANGE YOUR MINDSET TO POSITIVE, JOYFUL AND PLAYFUL.

- - -

Uncertainty

The markets will do whatever they want to do, nothing can be predicted with a 100% certainty. We learn to use high probable methods with at least 70% success results to reach our goals. We have been taught not make mistakes, we have conditioned our minds to only predict when we have certainty, but in the stock market nothing is certain we just train our minds to look at high probable successful outcomes, minimizing our loses, maximizing our games.

Worry

If you feel that you can't control that outcome of a trade then worry may begin to creep in. Your imagination starts to project bad outcomes so your mind becomes a worry machine and you become traumatized by worrying. By trading low price stocks with proper money management and proper diversification you minimize the worry. In my definition that includes everything between 1 and 8 dollars. The reason why we like the under eight dollar stock is because the big boys do not play in that arena. The reason we don't like under

$1 stocks which is sometimes called "Penny Stocks" is because generally there is too much hype in that market. The institutions and the hedge funds usually ignore these markets until the stocks trade over eight dollars a share. THATS WHY WE GUARD OUR TRADING ZONE WITH POSITIVE AND JOYFUL THOUGHTS AND FEELINGS.

Fear

Fear is when thoughts cause your mind to panic or freeze. Beneath all our fears are self-limiting beliefs. We have a sense of inadequacy like, "I will never be good enough," or "I'll never be smart enough." We have a sense of not mattering, or being unworthy or we are simply powerless in thinking that nothing I do will make a difference. By DECing your negative beliefs and receiving help and also by becoming a member of a like minded trading community this will lead you to better results. Our audio and videos on our website will help with this. WE TEACH TRADERS HOW TO SMILE, BREATHE DEEPLY AND FEEL JOYFUL TO COUNTERACT THIS.

Fears that traders have at the moment of trading:

We're now going to DEC our self-limiting beliefs behind our fears (in the next section we'll explain to you step-by-step). Delete – erase- and clear is written down on a piece of paper your fears. Then, you will erase those fears and replace them with a positive action word. An even easier way to do this is to type it out on a computer. Print it off and then delete the document you typed out. Later on in the book, this process will be more explain in depth.

If you have any sense of inadequacy that you will never be good enough because you make mistakes: delete, erase and clear (DEC). If you have any sense of not mattering to anyone: delete, erase and clear. If you have any sense of being unworthy: delete, erase and clear.

We are going to handle all of your fears about trading. If you're having any certainty or any hesitations about pulling the trigger: delete, erase and clear. If you have a fear of loss, or pulling the trigger: delete, erase and clear. If you have a fear on missing out, on the impulse trade or something else: delete, erase and clear. If you have any fears of not being right or making mistakes: delete, erase and clear. If you have any fears on an accuracy: delete, erase and clear. If you have any fears of self-sabotage: delete, erase and clear. Fears on blowing up your account: delete, erase and clear. Any fear of success or any fear of failure or anything involved with money and trading: delete, erase and clear. If you have any fear of growth or change or coming out of your comfort zone: delete, erase and clear.

Anything that will hold you back of having the courage to trade: delete, erase and clear.

Your fears about your trading that are based in your subconscious: delete, erase and clear. Anything that is preventing you from retraining your brain-mind connection with trading; delete, erase and clear.

Eighty percent of trading is in your head. IF I HAD TO PICK JUST ONE THING TO CHANGE IT WOULD BE TRADERS INNER MIND. Anything that's preventing you from your mind to be a performance trader: delete, erase and clear. Anything that's preventing you from being able to visualize correctly: delete, erase and clear. Anything that's preventing you from clearly knowing what you want: delete, erase and clear. Anything that's stopping you from being in the flow of being a good performance trader and having balance in your life: delete, erase and clear.

LET YOUR PAST MAKE YOU BETTER NOT BITTER.

Anything that's preventing you from following your dreams, staying focused, having your true vision, to reassure your beliefs: delete, erase and clear. Anything that's preventing you from not knowing the most powerful muscle (your mind) of knowing what you want: delete, erase and clear. Anything that's preventing you from mastering your inner game as a trader: delete, erase and clear.

Remember, what separates the best tennis players from the rest of the field? They all have the best equipment, they have the best sponsors, they all have countless hours of practice, they all have tremendous coaches perfecting their craft, they all know how to get the ball they know how to position themselves. So what separates the tennis players from the rest of the crowd? They all know how to do it. But when the money is on the line in the clutch, they perform.

How are you going to organize yourself and your subconscious mind to have good performance? How are you going to trade using your emotions in trading and thinking positively to reach your optimum results? REPLACING YOUR NEGATIVES WITH SOMETHING ELSE MUST BE MIXED WITH FEELINGS OF BLISS WITH THE NEW THOUGHTS.

- - -

In trading, people have a fear of failure and a fear of success. Take 3-5 minutes and clearly imagine and then write on a piece of paper your fears of success and fears of failures. What will your life be like if you release your deeply rooted trading fears? What good emotions will you experience? Get a clear mental image of what that looks like and then do the same with your fears of success about life and trading. What we are trying to create is a new trading brain that has DECed its negatives, visualized a new trading future in the alpha state and anchoring that new behavior to your new trading brain. PEOPLE ALWAYS DO WHAT IS MOST NORMAL TO THEM. SO TAKE A FEW MINUTES TO ASK YOURSELF SOME TOUGH QUESTIONS.

You might say to yourself, *"I don't have any fears of success and failure."* I'm going to list a series of statements and if any of them make sense or resonate with you, you want to DEC them and replace them with positive affirmations.

The list is:

1. Are there any fears of being lonely in trading or lonely being at the top?
2. Keeping and maintaining the successful trading you are going to have.
3. People diffusing rumors about you because you only sit at home in front of computer making money.
4. Maybe deep down you feel like you are not good enough to follow the system.
5. Maybe you think you won't be able to keep up with the constant changes of the market.
6. Feeling unworthy because you are receiving things you want from the profits of trading.
7. Earning money sitting in front of your computer while in your pajamas.
8. Your friends or family members may begin to abandon you because you don't have the normal everyday problems.

EVERYWHERE IN NATURE WE SEE EVIDENCE OF ABUNDANCE LOOK AT THE MARKET THAT WAY.

On our website (penniestothousands.com), in the future, we will have subconscious downloads available. It will consist of special harmonic music and layered positive suggestions. BOTH MALE AND FEMALE SUGGESTIONS. The audios will consist of music that can be played while you are trading to keep you in a traders zone. We will also have an alpha recording with scientifically proven beats and special programmed music with 4D holographic suggestions. ALL DIGITAL HELP WILL BE ABSORBED FASTER WITH EMOTIONS OF BLISS AND JOY- THIS HAS BEEN PROVEN WITH RESEARCH DONE AT A MAJOR UNIVERSITY.

These can be played at night and while you are trading. They will help you DEC your fears of success or fears of failure. It will have special music to help you program positive affirmations and positive visualizations. THIS WILL HELP YOUR PERSONAL TRADERS ZONE TO EXPERIENCE BLISS AND JOY.

I also suggest that you keep a daily trading journal of your feelings and emotions of your successes and failures. And I suggest that after you finish writing in your trading journal and discover any weaknesses, you review these with our special audios. ALSO NOTING YOUR JOYFUL ACTIVITY.

- - -

Developing the mind to become a successful trader.

Changing self-limiting beliefs require subconscious changes. We are going to teach you how to delete negative thinking. Many people have limited beliefs about trading and money. We are going to teach you how to identify your most damaging money blocks. We are going to clear your negative responses towards trading money and your living environment. These negative blocks may have cost you thousands of dollars over your lifetime. I am going to teach you a simple way to erase these negative experiences subconsciously or consciously.

We are going to use a simple technique to eliminate all your false beliefs about money and trading. We'll provide you tools and exercises to work on your beliefs about trading and money, and take you through powerful money cleaning sessions. EVERYTHING MENTIONED HERE IS BACKED UP BY THE LATEST SCIENTIFIC RESEARCH.

The first thing you have to do is to get a notebook. A three subject notebook will be the best. Open your subconscious thoughts about money or trading. Set your goals on what you hope to achieve by trading low price stocks. Now, bring all your negative thoughts about money and trading to the forefront. Writing your thoughts down reinforces your thoughts.

Let's begin a profitable new journey in making money. Where do you wish to be at the end of this book? Would you like money to flow to you automatically? Would you like to end procrastination and move forward in your trading? Would you like to be aware of and remove your financial and trading blocks? Every choice you make has a subconscious energy frequency to it.

The first rule you have to follow is that you have to give yourself permission to be playful. PAYING ATTENTION TO THINGS THAT MAKE YOU FEEL JOYFUL. The first rule about playfulness is to not trade with real money. Play with paper money which you can get from **AmeriTrade**. Be willing to change, be willing to see the positive results from your trading. Make a new choice. We want profits to flow to you. We want you to stop beating yourself up. Develop a money intuition. We are going to get rid of your negative ideas about it.

We are going to use a system called **DEC**.

Delete
Erase
Clear

We want to say it three times so your subconscious believes that you mean it. For example: let's take a common belief that people have about trading. A lot of people feel that if I trade at my desk at home I'm really not working. But in reality, if you trade well you can make profits and have a dream life with lots of freedom.

You can be abundant and things can change. So let's take this first statement. Write the following statement in a notebook or type it on your computer: "*Trading is not a real job.*"

If it's written on a piece of paper, erase it and replace it with a statement that is positive for your subconscious mind like: "*Trading is a very profitable way of life, it will give me my dream life and it will give me freedom with my family.*" If you typed it on your computer simply hit the delete button and type the new positive statement. Throughout this book we will delete all the falsehoods about trading and money.

Remember: truth feels light, lies feel dense. JOY FEELS GOOD, WORRY FEELS HEAVY, THINGS WILL CHANGE SHORTLY.

Start thinking about how you can change your feelings about your financial situation. We need to clear all doubt and fear from your trading system. So grab your notebook or your computer and bring your negatives to your forefront. SHIFT YOUR TRADER MINDSET. BUILD A NEW TRADE ZONE.

Maybe you think you are too old or too young. Maybe you think it is not for me or it is for somebody else. Perhaps you think you are not smart enough. Maybe you don't believe you can do it. Maybe you believe you lack the ability. Maybe you simply believe it will never happen to me. You practice self-sabotage.

If you have any doubts at all just call a CAB. This is an acronym I have created to help you remember what to do once the fear and self-doubts start creeping into your mind. **C** stands for being **concise** with details and actions and being cleared of all negative beliefs. **A** stands for **asking** with total belief. **B** stands for that **belief** coming to you but without a deadline and allowing IT to bring you what you want. You need to call your CAB in a happy state, not waiting for your future intention to arrive. A great example to relate to is when a farmer plants seeds for the next season he plants them in fertile soil (the happy mind) and he knows without a doubt that they will grow. He doesn't stand around waiting to see if they have grown or not because he knows that by the end of the season he will have a full crop. As you take actions toward your goals become like the farmer, asking the universe for your wants but not standing around waiting for it to come wondering why it's not happening sooner. YOUR INNER MIND RESPONDS TO REPETITIVE JOYFUL INTENTIONS.

Below are some sample questions to ask yourself if you are holding on to any false beliefs that may be helping you function today but you no longer need to believe.

Question No. 1: What identities have you attached to your money?

Question No. 2: Are you afraid to fail?

Question No. 3: What does your family want from you?

Question No. 4: Do you have any fundamental negative beliefs about money? For example: money has to be earned.

Question No. 5: Have you failed at something recently?

Question No. 6: Are you not aware of the action plan to take?

Question No. 7: What is preventing you to have profits in trading?

Question No. 8: What is the most negative influence in your trading?

So go to your notebook or computer. Pay attention to the answers to your questions. Now DEC them and remember the formula. Delete, Erase, Clear. DEC IT! DEC IT! And after you delete them from your computer change them to a positive present and future statement and make sure you avoid negative words. **ALWAYS CHANGE THE NEGATIVE WORDS TO POSITIVE.** POSITIVE MUST BE FOLLOWED WITH PLAYFUL JOYFUL FEELINGS. Try to bring in positive emotions and visualizations. If you have a problem doing it, as some people do, try to add in details and build out the picture.

GO AND WAKE UP YOUR MIND TO LUCK.

The next section is is a series of sample questions to help you remove any negative associations about trading:

Question No. 1: Are you avoiding paper work?

Question No. 2: Do you keep an active daily trading journal?

Question No. 3: Do you have any other fears of success?

Question No. 4: Are you scared to try?

Question No. 5: Are you avoiding pain?

Question No. 6: Are you learning from your mistakes?

Question No. 7: What is your trading style teaching you today?

Question No. 8: Are you practicing good money management techniques?

LIVE AND TRADE STRESS FREE AND UNSHAKEABLE.

Once again write the answers of these questions in your notebook, paper or computer. DEC them out with a positive statement and positive emotions. You must do this three times. The first time your mind doesn't take it seriously. The second time it begins to focus more energy on the statement. And the third time your mind believes you are serious. SHARE YOUR MOTIVATIONAL THOUGHTS ON OUR SOCIAL MEDIA. SHARE INSPIRATION DAILY.

- - -

This next section consists of a series of questions to examine yourself.

Question No. 1: Look at the kinds of words you are using to describe things.
Question No. 2: What is your worst enemy in your life?
Question No. 3: Are you afraid of being great and making profits?
Question No. 4: Do you procrastinate? Do you have unfinished projects?

DEC any of the negative answers to these questions on your computer (three times) and complete them with a positive charging statement.

Now write down some positive questions. Here are some examples:

Question 1: What do I need to do to make more profits on my trading?

Question 2: Do I need a pilots checklist before I trade?

Question 3: What do I need to allow a dream life in trading and enjoy my life with my family?

Question 4: What do I need to do to create a good energy to have unlimited profits on my trading? HAVE FUN IN YOUR TRADING LIFE.

Any other positive questions you have write them out or type them on your computer. DEC any questions that have negative answers.

We are going to DEC any fear of change and learning to let go. So grab your notebook again or your computer and be open to any positive awareness. Set your goals on what you hope to achieve. Bring your negative thoughts to the forefront.

What I want you to do is close your eyes and imagine there is a bright light high above you and imagine that this brilliant energy is flowing into your mind. When you feel that energy going through your body imagine it penetrating every cell, nerve, tissue and fiber of your body. I want you to feel or see this source helping you to know what you need to do. Close your eyes. Then I want you to take a deep breath. Hold it and exhale twice as long as you inhaled, visualizing or feeling the energy above you and I want you to feel it going from your head down to the tip of your toes.

I want you to breathe deeply through your nose and hold it. Then exhale through your mouth breathing out all the negative energy. When you breathe in this energy source anchor it with something physical like snapping your fingers, putting your index fingers together or anything that will anchor it. I want you to feel it or see it bringing about new ideas, thoughts or life changes. Bringing new information or skills allow your energy to receive new ideas. MAKE

IT PLAYFUL, BRING IT, SMILING, LAUGHING AND JOYFUL FEELINGS.

You should DEC them three times and replace them with positive emotions statements. Once again grab that notebook or computer. Be open to positive changes. Set your goals on what you hope to achieve and get ready to continue on your abundant new journey. We are going to start asking ourselves what things can bring us more abundance in our trading.

The following are personal health questions you should ask yourself:

Question 1: How can I get more sleep?
Question 2: What can I do to keep mind and body in good shape?
Question 3: What can I do to keep my family happy and not bother me when I'm trading?
Question 4: What things can I be grateful for? For example: Things you can be grateful for are: your beautiful home, your lovely family, your nice computer, your money accounts, your good health or simple things like your life, food, shelter, love, pets or this trading system. There are many things to be grateful for.

Learn to practice the art of gratitude in your life, in your children/grandchildren/partner and in your trading. I AM VISUALIZING POSITIVE WITH BLISSFUL FEELINGS.

Many people have ideas about money that are linked to their family and we want to DEC the ones you have. You're going to write all the negative thoughts you have about money and your family, but first I'm going to give you some sample thoughts:

Thought 1: Dad/mom didn't have much money so I can't...

Thought 2: My parents always fought about money so I must have a conflict about money.

Thought 3: I'm not worthy to be loved.

Thought 4: I can't keep wealth or trust it.

Thought 5: Making money is hard.

Thought 6: My abundance will take away from other people's wealth.

Thought 7: Nothing works for me.

Thought 8: My spouse never supports me.

Thought 9: Everyone does it better.

Thought 10: Lack of money makes me more spiritual.

ETC...REMEMBER FEEL LIKE YOUR FLOWING IN ABUNDANCE IN YOUR PERSONAL TRADING ZONE.

Remember from the time we are small to when we get older we collect negative beliefs from those we love. At that time it was not intended to harm us but unfortunately we have held on to those false beliefs. Now we must learn to forgive those people who gave us those beliefs. NEW BELIEFS WILL BE ADOPTED FASTER WITH THE RIGHT JOYFUL EMOTIONS.

Now that you have learned the importance to forgive others and let go of your false beliefs we are ready to move on the next phase. SELF GROWTH WITH TRADING WILL LEAD TO YOUR PERSONAL FULFILLMENT.

Write down your individual things that will help you become a better trader.

We need to clear the fear of success. Look at the things or needs you have to be a good disciplined trader. Trading gives me whatever I require. This is what I require. WHAT IT MEANS IS THAT YOUR BRAIN IS PLIABLE LIKE PLASTIC. YOU CAN CHANGE YOUR MIND AND OVERCOME YOUR FINANCIAL BLOCKS.

So ask yourself these questions: *What do I need to do to build my dream life with trading ? How can I be grateful for all the things trading brings to me?*

We need to clear any fear of numbers or goals we have, so let's come up with a number that you feel comfortable in earning in profits in trading every month (start with small numbers as it will help you with your belief system that will help with larger numbers later). APPRECIATE MONEY AND ITS USES

If this is a very large number break it down to small numbers, or small numbers first. In this book you will learn different trading styles with low price stocks that will help you achieve your goals, thus the title of the book, "Pennies into Thousands". We are going to ask you some questions about your monthly financial goals:

Question No. 1: What am I avoiding that is not allowing me to reach this goal?

Question No. 2: What conditions am I placing on trading that are blocking from me from my profits?

Questions No. 3: What rules am I not following?

Question No. 4: What drama am I living to block my trading profits?

Question No. 5: What am I avoiding or refusing to see about trading?

DEC your answers three times — which means: delete, erase and clear — and rewrite a positive statement in present tense with as much emotional and vibrational energy you can put into the statements. Use alpha state music in the background to help you. There are many free alpha-states music in YouTube. Repeat and reread out loud every day. Write down your monthly target and put it on your trading desk or download the free app by Jack Canfield, "Vision Board", which you can download for free on Android or Apple. Put on the vision board your monthly trading target and any pictures you have from your photo. Also, the application allows you to download pictures from the internet to help you with your goals.

There is also an audio part to this application that you can use "I am" statements. These statements must be short, simple, and in the present tense as it only allows you three seconds to record. Some people have a problem placing something after an "I am" statement because they don't believe it. In this case, place "I am in the process of." For example, I am in the process of becoming a great trader. I am in the process of losing weight. Remember linking emotions with your positive "I'm going to" or "I'm" mill increase the velocity of your success. THINGS LIKE I AM ENTERING VIP TRADING CLUB.

Write this underneath: I manifest this number in my trading life and everything not allowing this to happen. I Delete, Erase and Clear it all (DEC). OVERCOME ALL OBSTACLES TO YOUR TRADING WEALTH. YOUR PROSPERITY IS IN YOUR HANDS.

Getting clear in your future life in trading

Try to visualize or feel the trading opportunities on your screen. Figure out what drives you, what helps you, what makes you happy enough to make good trading decisions. I WANT YOU TO BE A GENIUS IN AFFIRMATIONS LOOKING ON HOW TO PUT AN EMOTIONAL HIGH IN MY AFFIRMATIONS.

Clear clutter out of your work space: do not prevent any clutter in your research area, on your desk or in your mind. Ask yourself what it is going to take to remove the clutter out of your life and trading area. CLUTTER AND NEGATIVE SHOULD BE AWAY FROM YOUR MIND AND YOUR WORKSPACE.

See yourself as the new you, the new trader you desire. Ask yourself this question: if you were an actor playing the role of a successful trader living your dream life, what features and qualities do you need to bring to this role? What personality traits do you require to get this life style? For example: adequate sleep, good nutrition, good research. IF I WAS IN YOUR TRADER ZONE I WOULD MAKE IT AS FUN AS YOU CAN.

Ask yourself if you can build the new trader you: what else do you need? How can I speed up my life as a trader and make it happen now? Do you give yourself permission to change? If not, why not? YOU MUST BE HAPPY WITH YOURSELF BEFORE YOU CAN REALLY BE HELP TO OTHERS.

I want you to end this cycle of sabotaging your trading now. You deserve the best in your trading, the absolute best in your life. I'm committed as your trading Buddha to help you and your trading success. I'd like you to join our trading community, which will continue giving you more and more keys to the abundance of trading and end your cycle of sabotage no matter how the market reacts. ASSOCIATE WITH THE PEOPLE AT THE LEVEL OF TRADING YOU WANT TO ACHIEVE.

We will clear all the beliefs that are holding you back from having all the success and abundance that you deserve from trading. We will work with the traders mind to align you with successful trading. The trader's mind means you're going to have loosing trades. Loosing trades are part of the trading business. You have to learn to lose good. You have to learn that when you lose you need to examine what went wrong and figure out what can you do different next time. You will always have losses but they can be small and your winnings big. PUT IN YOUR MIND YOU DESERVE MORE WINNERS THAN LOSERS.

You're going to learn from this book and our trading community how to turn on your money magnet and profits in trading. You're going to wake up your prosperity subconscious to a mind of prosperity. By deleting your negative beliefs you are waking up your prosperous subconscious mind.

As you're becoming more confident in clearing your old beliefs and programming, you release your doubts and fears and become more powerful from anything that has been holding you back from your trading abundance.

"We are what we pretend to be"

—Kurt Vonnegut.

Do you think you can make that commitment of 3 minutes a day? To put your success on auto-pilot for trading? You prove by buying this book or joining our website that you're a person of action and it shows the commitment to get in touch with your trading goals of your dreams and in your life. Ultimately your subconscious you will choose to invest your time and energy and that is when you'll see results. DID YOU KNOW THAT THE SIMPLE ACT OF SETTING PROPER TRADING GOALS FOR YOURSELF ACTIVATES GENIUS PART OF YOUR BRAIN.

I'm asking 3 minutes in the morning to DEC your negative beliefs and 3 minutes at night, you're DECing reposition with positive trading ideas. But by investing 6 minutes a day, on a consistent basis, it will attract to your trading intuition to your traders mind, the trading engineering mind. By using my systems you can bring in the dollars you want. Even if it's a small amount everyday it's more consistent than not doing it at all.

People say to me, *"Mike, that sounds great to get rid of my negative trading beliefs and I have an idea that this DEC will make a change in my trading style on my psychology and let me be successful. But I don't really understand the technology or it seems all so far out right brain. I'm a little worried how it is going to impact my life."* Don't worry about technology. Your subconscious mind has always been running 90% of your life. Your subconscious is attracting you to the right ideas and to the right prosperity for trading.

Then, you have the systems which I call the engineering part/ left brain part. The truth is that any subconscious programming or subconscious technology used in your mind is very simple in scientific process, proving to be very powerful. The first real change is a subconscious change and a subconscious believe linked with positive emotions. The stronger the emotion, the stronger the vibration. BE THE UP YOU THE JOYFUL, THE FUN YOU.

When you help clear space, clear the negative beliefs and attitudes out of your mind. The positive, rebalancing, will actually be more absorbed into your conscious and help you trade with our new systems. We want nothing to hold you back. Your trader's mind will become conditioned to see opportunities for success and trading during every trading moment of your day. All you have to do is practice your DEC like I told you. THE EXCITEMENT GENERATED BY VISUALIZING AFTER DECING HELPS YOUR MOTIVATION TO TAKE ACTION. THEN IN YOUR TRADERZONE THE PART OF YOUR MIND THAT CREATES ANXIETY GETS TURNED OFF.

If you don't get rid of the old ones use our DEC method and eliminate this old physical, mental, financial, sociable, type of negative beliefs you have.

By DECing your old beliefs you are allowing prosperity. You'll help to quickly and safely rewire this internal programing you have for unlimited success in your trading ability.

That's one of the biggest reasons why this system is so unbelievably powerful. But don't worry, you don't have to be a scientist or an engineer to understand it. You don't have to understand the technology to receive the benefits. Just do what I say and remember that when you change your old beliefs, your subconscious mind will believe in prosperity, money and trading. Your life will shift, and your new trading style will give you new endless profitable possibilities. I AM WHAT I WANT TO BE.

- - -

Clearing self-sabotage

Are you living in emotional ease? Are you doing fun things for yourself?

Remember that with all these questions you have to DEC it three times and create a new statement that is positive, in the present tense, and full of good energy. What do you have to do to create a financial trading plan to be disciplined with it and to act on it?

Are you angry about losing trades? Or are you learning from them?

Here are some statements and questions that you might want to DEC:

- I don't have advanced degrees or a special career.
- Am I willing to learn new strategies to learn a different way of trading that consistently brings me profits?
- Sitting in front of a computer at home is not a job.
- Do I know my financial roadblocks?
- Do I understand my money blueprint on my subconscious? We've got to clear those negative beliefs. We've got to DEC them: Delete, Erase and clear. Replace them with some positive energy, including the present and looking to the future.

EXAMPLES OF AFFIRMATIONS:

I AM FEARLESS WITH MY TRADING I CAN LAUGH AT MY MISTAKES

I AM WISE WHEN PREPARING TO TRADE

I AM GUARDING MY TRADE ZONE WITH JOY

I AM DELETING ALL MY NEGATIVE BELIEFS

I AM LEARNING FROM ALL MY MISTAKES

I KNOW MY WEAKNESSES AND SHIFTING TO POSITIVE

I AM JOYFUL WITH MY TRADING RESULTS

I AM ALLOWING EXPERTS AND PEOPLE TO HELP ME

EVERY DAY IN EVERY WAY I AM BECOMING A BETTER TRADER

I AM SLEEPING BETTER AND SOUNDER

I AM SMILING MORE WHEN I TRADE

I AM STIMULATING MY BRAIN TO TRADE BETTER

I AM TRUSTING MYSELF TO MAKE GOOD DECISIONS

I AM OPEN TO POSSIBILITY

I AM TRADING ACCOUNT FLOWING WITH MONEY

MONEY COMES EASILY TO ME

I AM BLESSED IN MY TRADING

I AM DOMINATING LOW PRICE STOCKS

I AM PRACTICING JOY IN MY PERSONAL TRADING LIFE

I AM MOVING AND BREATHING AT MY TRADERS AREA

I AM FACING MY FEARS WITH GRATITUDE

I AM GIVING THANKS FOR ALL MY TRADING CONQUESTS

I AM DRINKING PLENTY OF WATER

I AM CHOOSING A JOYFUL AND HAPPY TRADING ZONE

I AM HAPPY I AM CHOOSING MY OWN COURSE

I AM ENJOYING THE OUTCOMES I BRING

I AM CONFIDENT

I AM FEELING GOOD OF MY DESIRES

I AM DOWNLOADING KNOWLEDGE WHEN I NEED IT

I AM IN THE TRADERS FLOW

I AM WINNING THE INNER GAME

I AM A LIFE FULL OF ABUNDANCE

I AM FINDING PEACE OF MIND IN ALL TOUGH SITUATIONS

I AM ALLOWING WEALTH AND WELL BEING

I AM IN ALIGNMENT WITH THE PERFECT TRADING ZONE

I AM GIVING COMPLIMENTS TO MYSELF AND OTHERS

I AM DOING A GOOD JOB OF TRADING

I AM HARMONY WITH MY TRADING STRATEGIES

I AM IN FLOW OF MONEY

MY POWER FOLLOWS MY INTENTIONS

I AM RECONDITIONING MY TRADERS MIND

I AM CRUSHING MY LIMITING BELIEFS

I AM PROPERLY IDENTIFYING PRICE MOMENTUM WITH PRECISION

I AM UNDERSTANDING FIBONACCI AND THE GOLDEN RATIO IN TRADING IMPORTANCE

I KNOW WHEN AND HOW TO PLACE STOP LOSSES

I AM USING CANDLESTICKS WITH TREND ANALYSIS

I AM ENTERING HIGH PROBABILITY OPPORTUNITIES WITH LIMITED RISK

I AM CREATING SUCESS IN ALL MY TRADING

I AM PROUD OF MY WINS AND I AM PUBLISHING THEM

I AM PASSIONATE ABOUT MY GOALS ANDI RESONATING WITH THEM ON A CORE LEVEL

I AM MAKING POSITIVE LASTING CHANGES

I AM BREATHING DEEPLY AND SLOWLY WHEN I TRADE

I DESERVE TO BE WEALTHY AND SUCCESSFUL IN TRADING

I FEEL INSPIRED AND MOTIVATED WHEN I TRADE

I DRAW OPPORTUNITIES TO TRADE TOWARD ME

I AM IN THE RIGHT STOCK AT THE RIGHT TIME

ABUNDANCE FLOWS FREELY TO ME

YOU ARE ACCEPTING ALL AFFIRMATIONS

ALL OF MY TRADING NEEDS ARE MET

I BELIEVE IN MYSELF

I LOVE BEING SUCCESSFUL

I AM APPROVING QUALITY OF MY LIFE

I AM GETTING GOOD RESULTS AS I BELIEVE IN MYSELF MORE

I AM CHOOSING MY BEST IDEAS

I AM UNLOCKING ALL MY POTENTIAL

I AM EXECUTING WELL

I AM JOYFULLY HAVING WEALTH

IT IS GREAT TO HAVE ADDED INCOME

MY BRAIN IS THE MACHINE THAT DRIVES MY LIFE

I AM HAVING ALL RESOURCES AT MY FINGERTIPS

WHAT WILL YOUR NEW RICH BRAIN FEEL LIKE

ITS MY JOY TO SHARE MY WEALTH

I AM POWERFUL AND CONTROL OF MY DESTINY

I AM OPEN TO ATTRACTING WEALTH

MY MIND IS MY BEST FRIEND

YOU ARE INNOVATIVE

I AM BECOMING A BETTER TRADER EVERY DAY

I AM BLUEPRINT FOR A GREAT LIFE

I AM PICKING STOCKS THAT ARE BIG WINNERS

I AM USING WORDS LIKE WIN

I RELEASE THE TRADING DRAMA OF MY PAST

I MATTER ON WHAT I HAVE TO OFFER

I AM READY TO ENJOY PROFITS

- - -

Use your vision board with these affirmations. It's better to start your intentions with I am. What you imagine in your mind and what you actually experience are the same thing.

University studies demonstrate that when a person imagines stress, the chemicals produced in the body are the same as real stress and vice versa.

- - -

Tips to build a good self-image for trading recognize small victories.

- Recognize small victories.
- Take responsibility for your current situation.
- Do something for others.
- Take baby steps to your final vision every day.
- Do not compare your performance to others.
- Change your limiting beliefs with decisions.

Based on my student emails and my teaching experience-blueprint for results. When you set a goal or intention and negative pop up, dec it at the moment. Your inner mind will be hit a tipping point, it will become effortless. Visualize your future with repetition, use details and action movement.

Two hundred studies have proven this: top performers in all fields use (if you have problems with seeing) your feelings, simply visualize the way you worry, just do it the opposite way, rehears internally first.

Shift your mind away from blaming others, own your life

Forgive yourself and others

Let the past go

Make lazy or joy time evert day

Paint your day before you fully wake up

Intuition gets better every day, like working out your muscles

21 days in a row will turn a habit

Gratitude is the key to experience joy, counting all your joys is magnetic

Trading journal is your path of self discovery not just in trading but in life

Write in your journal, write our your DECS, your goals, your reasons and your bliss. In time it will become natural

Trading is a never ending process

Invest in yourself, things will always change

There is no punctuation with these thoughts because I want them to just flow

"People who are unable to motivate themselves must be content with mediocrity, no matter how impressive their other talents"

- Andrew Carnegie

Questions and answers with Dr. Kluzinski

1. Do I really have to read my new positive statements out loud?
   — Yes, in the beginning you do. By reading them out loud they will be imprinted on your subconscious mind.

2. Do I really need to DEC (Delete, Erase, Clear) from my subconscious three times?
   — Yes, your subconscious is 90% of your mind and your conscious is 10%. By DECing your negative statements three times your subconscious will pay attention to what you are doing. With only one time your subconscious believes that you are not serious.

3. If any statement feels heavy or negative to me should I DEC it more than three times?
   — Yes, DEC it five or eight times to help clear the financial negative statements from your blueprint with positive emotions.

4. Do my bad trading experiences OR MONRY EXPERIENCES from the past affect me?
   — Yes, it does. That's why you need to write down or on your computer all past negative experiences with trading and DEC them to replace them with positive statements.

5. Do my friends opinions affect me?
   — They shouldn't but they do. Thus, any of your close friends that have negative opinion about your

trading please write them down. Then DEC them and replace them with a positive statement. THERE IS RESEARCH THAT SAYS YOU ARE AN AVERAGE OF THE 5 PEOPLE YOU SPEND THE MOST TIME WITH.

6. Does my family opinion affect my trading?
— Absolutely, these are the people that are closest to you. These are the people that have put negative imprints in your mind from day one. Thus all your negative statements you have to read out loud, put them in your computer or notebook and DEC them.

7. Isn't all trading conscious mind decisions?
— The creators of trading systems would like you to believe that, but in reality most good traders have created a good subconscious mind for trading. They're known as trading in a zone.

8. Do most people lose when they trade?
— Yes, more people lose than win. That's because they have bad subconscious beliefs, bad discipline, poor work habits or a bad trading system.

9. How can I minimize the chance of losing when I trade?
a. Have good subconscious beliefs about money and trading.
b. Start off by trading without PAPER money. This will give you a chance to gain some experience in my trading indicators and charts.

c. Another way to minimize is to diversify your portfolio in small stocks. You should put no more than 5% in any stock and no more than 2 to 3 stocks in any industry. **Only trade with money you can afford to lose.**

10. Are there any other beliefs I should be aware of?
— Yes, any beliefs you generally have about money or earning money. For example: If you believe that trading stocks is not a real job then you will find a way to sabotage your profits. If your parents believe that you need to go to a factory or an office to earn money then you will sabotage your trading ability. If your spouse or significant other should put the belief in your mind that you have to leave your house to earn money then you could sabotage yourself in trading in your home in front of a computer.

11. Can I trade part time?
— Yes, there are many ways of trading before or after the markets and during certain periods of the day. You could stop and limit orders so you don't need to be in front of a computer all day long. WE TEND TO GET CAUGHT UP IN EVERYDAY ACTIVITIES. WHAT ABOUT 10 OR 20 YEARS FROM NOW? THE BEST TIME TO START EVEN IF ITS PART TIME IS NOW.

12. Any other negative beliefs I should be aware of?
— Yes, any beliefs you have about your negative self esteem will always affect your trading ability.

Thus you should DEC it and replace it for a positive statement.

13. Is trading a process?

— Yes, in the beginning you will have negative beliefs and make stupid mistakes. But if you keep a trading journal your subconscious beliefs will get stronger over a period of time and you will become a better trader. You will notice after trading for a while, you will make less mistakes and you will have a better subconscious belief system about yourself and trading. The higher the belief you have about successful thoughts you will have higher levels of success. Just remember that you will always have loosing trades. Just keep the amounts small.

14. Do I have to believe in metaphysical energy or have strong religious belief?

— No, absolutely not. You just have to open you mind -assist you in clearing your negative statements. Whatever that has to be it doesn't matter the style of belief you just have to leave your mind open to a higher energy. PEACE AND JOY ARE THE GOAL OF MOST HUMAN BEINGS. CHASING AFTER MONEY IS ENERGIZED IF YOU FEEL THE RESULTS WILL MAKE YOU HAPPY OR HELP OTHERS.

15. Why don't other trading books deal with your subconscious beliefs?

— Trading is a whole brain process. There are very good books on the psychology of trading but most books deal with a system of trading. I have a PHD in finance and experience with behavior psychology. I have combined both the psychological and the trading system to be a successful trader. You must learn to develop your left and right side of your brain to be a good trader. Over time it will become naturally easier while you are making your profits. Remember, discipline is a strong trait to have while trading.

16. Many people tell me, *"I can't visualize very well. I write things down and I do the clearing but I can't visualize well. I use affirmations but my brain keeps bringing up negative things especially before I trade."*

"You have to think anyway, so why not think big"

- Donald Trump.

— Play the 21 second game. What is that? First, 21 is a Fibonacci number so whatever your goal or program is give me 21 seconds and think about it. For example: let's say you're visualizing on a special car. For 21 seconds drench your senses and everything about that car. See yourself driving it, going fast, touching the leather, playing with the buttons, listening to the music. Look at the color, see the shapes, look at the decals, and see yourself with the people you love in there. For 21 seconds use **ALL YOUR SENSES** and nothing else. Don't think of anything else for 21 seconds and flood your mind for that time. AFTER 21 SECONDS THESE THOUGHTS WILL ATTRACT OTHER GOOD THOUGHTS.

17. Is it possible that one powerful trading system and clearing your subconscious consistently beat the markets?

— **Yes**, by clearing, affirming and visualizing, we can cut through all the noise and we can consistently find profitable winning trades and cut losses quickly. I have found that after someone has looked at charts over and over they develop a sixth sense by using my indicators to pick winners. The number I have found is at least 10,000 charts. You may say, *"Well Michael, 10,000 seems like a lot,"* but it really isn't because if you look at 40 charts a day x 5 days a week = 200. If you look at charts 4 weeks a month then you are looking at 800. If I look at 12 months you will have looked at more than 10,000 charts. So that means in a years time you will have developed a better sense of being a great technical trader. Trading is an evolution. YOUR INNER MIND IS ON A ONGOING JOURNEY OF GOOD RESULTS.

18. Many of you become so concentrated on trading that you ignore the people closest around you. We will give a kind a suggestion: When you are spending time with people, whether it be at breakfast or dinner, just ask 2 questions:

— Bring some positivity and say: What did you see today that was positive? Bring a positive subject and be kind.

Then in the conversation work in the second question, which is:

— What have you done recently that you have not been appreciated or recognized for? Everybody's looking for recognition, everybody's looking for appreciation. You're looking to improve the relationships in your life by improving this. As you improve your trading mind you will improve your trading results.

You have to practice. The more you practice, the more consistent you will be.

I want you to get as much specific maximum benefit out of this DEC training session and help you restart your tremendous trading life. I want you to effortlessly attract the wealth you desire, to be able to go after the opportunities, know the right indicators, and not be scared anymore. I want you to feel confident on your new level of passion in trading. I highly recommend that you take a few minutes and review this chapter before going on to the rest of the book.

TRADING IS NOT LIKE THE MOVIES DIVIDED INTO GENRES. THERE WILL BE GREAT DAYS,TRAGIC DAYS,COMICAL DAYS, AND YES ONCE IN A WHILE HORRIFYING DAYS.

2

FIBONACCI NUMBERS

HOW A MATH WIZ BORN IN THE 12TH CENTURY IN ITALY, EDUCATED IN NORTH AFRICA, SON OF A DIPLOMAT HELPED MY FINANCIAL LIFE.

What is a Fibonacci number?

The simple definition is when added together it equals the next number.

The Fibonacci numbers are: 1, 1, 2, 3, 5, 8, 13, 21, 34, 55 and so on. In my indicators that I use I always try to use a Fibonacci number, but sometimes the numbers that I use in the charts are not Fibonacci numbers.

Why is that? The reason is that I believe you should use the Fibonacci whenever possible but you have to be aware of all the other traders in the market and the numbers they use. For example, if I have 50 day moving average and 200 day moving average you will notice that these are not Fibonacci numbers but are the levels that all the other traders are using. You have to be aware of them and whenever possible use Fibonacci numbers.

Fibonacci sequence appeared centuries ago in the SanScript Writings. In the west, the Fibonacci sequence first appeared around 1,200 AD.

This book is not a book about Fibonacci numbers but I am giving you a basic understanding which you can use in your trading. The Fibonacci sequence appears everywhere in nature from cows to bees, to sea shell shapes, branching plants, flower pedals, pineapples, apples and leaf arrangements.

The Fibonacci numbers are nature's numbering system and appear everywhere. Plants do not know about the sequence, they just grow in the most efficient ways. That is why I use Fibonacci numbers whenever I can.

I like to use Fibonacci numbers especially in replacements and extensions. For example, let's say a number for my indicator was 14. I might change it to 13 because 13 is a Fibonacci number and 14 isn't.

There is a popular opinion that when Fibonacci tools are used they can predict market behavior 70% of the time and in my philosophy if something works 70% of the time it is a rule for me because there is nothing that is a 100% certain in the market. Most trading platforms, like Traders View and Think or Swim, contain the tool for Fibonacci retracements or extensions.

If you have problems figuring out how to use the retracements or extensions in whatever platform you choose, Youtube has good explanation videos about these processes. Thus you don't have to know the precise mathematical formula just use the tool on your platform.

However, Fibonacci studies don't provide a mathematical tool for all traders. There is one tool in your tool box to help you make good trading decisions so when you think of trading think of a carpenter who has many tools in his tool box. He may need to use a combination of tools to finish the job and that is why we use a combination of indicators like tools to figure out our good trading decisions.

The Fibonacci method should only be used with other methods and the results derived should be considered as another decision point for you. For example, in this book we are going to use Fibonacci numbers in combination with William's Percentage R, which is a William's indicator, and CCI. These will all be explained in a further chapter.

We will also combine this with the five and twenty-one moving average and the fifty and two-hundred day moving average which are not Fibonacci numbers but all traders look at these numbers. Thus if all traders look at them then we should look too. For example, a retracement of a stock price of a certain percentage may alert a trader to a potential trend reversal or something. If you have a stock in a strong up trend you may be looking for a good price to enter, maybe that price is the 38.5% retracement of the last swing low to swing high.

The three key retracements that traders look for are 38.2%, 50% and 61.8%. You don't have to memorize this, there will be a tool in your charts and we will use these tools in combination with other tools. Both traders and investors have trouble finding good price levels to enter the market or where to place their stops or extensions. Thus, using Fibonacci retracements sometimes is a good price point to start to enter a trade. Stocks will often pull back or retrace a percentage of their previous move. When you are choosing you stocks under the $8 range a good place to choose the first exit position to take 50% of the table might be one of the Fibonacci extensions. Thus we can use our system that we are going to talk about later in the book to enter the trade and the Fibonacci extension as one of the exits along with our 8 Exponential Moving Average goal line.

FIB NUMBERS ARE FASCINATING GREAT KNOWLEDGE IS AVAILABLE ON THE INTERNET.-

THE PHI FREQUENCY IS ALSO KNOWN AS THE GOLDEN RATIO AND IT IS SEEN IN ANCIENT GEOMETRY THE PHI FREQUENCY IS THOUGHT TO BE A FUNDAMENTAL FREQUENCY. THE PHI FREQUENCY IS SEEN IN THE DESIGN OF THE GREAT PYRAMIDS IN GIZA. ALL OUR DIGITAL PRODUCTS CALIBRATE THIS IN OUR SOFTWARE WITH SPECIAL BEATS THAT COPY THIS PHI FREQUENCY.

WE ALSO USE SOUND IN OUR DIGITAL PRODUCTS CALLED BRAINWAVE ENTRAINMENT WHICH IS THE PRACTICE THAT AIMS TO CAUSE BRAINWAVE FREQUENCIES TO FALL INTO STEP WITH A PERIODIC STIMULUS. WE ALSO USE THE LATEST SCIENCE OF CREATIVE VISUALIZATION. WE INCORPORATE THE METHODS OF INNER MIND SYSTEMS TO INFUSE YOUR TRADER DREAMS AND DESIRES WITH PROPER ENERGY TO ENTER YOUR REALM OF REALITY FAST. THIS WILL WILL HELP TAP THE POWER THAT LIES WITH YOU.

"Success is not a fantasy, it's a mathematical formula"

3

LOW COST STOCKS UNDER $8

"THE PERSON THAT TURNS OVER THE MOST ROCKS WINS THE GAME. AND THAT IS MY PHILOSOPHY"—PETER LYNCH

It's simple. They are low price and they have the potential for big profits. A $2 stock to make a 100% only has to go to $4. But trading low cost stocks is also a good way to lose money. I'm not talking about low price stocks that get hyped with no good fundamentals. I'm not talking about stocks that get promoted by stock crooked promoters. In reality low price stocks got bashed by the media because people don't understand them or are too scared to trade them. Low cost stocks are mainly a misunderstood investment that people avoid for the wrong reasons.

Look at this information from Harvard University in 1997. There were reported losses of 1.3 billion dollars on stocks that were determined safe. Now consider that Harvard has some of the finest

PHD'S and geniuses advising them and they still lost over a billion dollars.

So you think that big stocks can't go bankrupt? Just look what happened to Harvard. These professional traders were supposed to know what they were doing. Low cost stocks are no more speculative than investments in great stocks. In fact, over the last 75 years low price stocks outperformed the blue chip industrial stocks.

In reality for me, low price stocks usually trade up to a value of $8 and just because the share price is low doesn't mean that the company is always risky. It is common to find low price stocks that have a lot of cash and high profit margins and are in good growth industries.

In www.tradingview.com, when you pay for the minimum subscription they allow you to make multiple watch-lists and save them. You can click between lists and monitor your candidates.

There are many platforms to monitor stocks, but for the simplicity of this book I'm going to use examples from this platform. I'm receiving no compensation from this platform You can click between lists and monitor your candidates.

> *"Only when the tide goes out do you discover who's been swimming naked."*
>
> *- Warren Buffett*

One list may be your A+ list. These are stocks that have met all the magic indicators above the Cloud, the 50 day moving average and are showing a good candlestick and don't have an Ichimoku Cloud on the weekly chart.

Then, you might create an A list. It might have stocks that have met all the daily indicators but are missing one or a few. In the weekly chart it might be below the cloud.

You might create a B list, which may contain all different price points. Trading View is a free web based trading platform but they do have multiple watch-lists that you can save data. But be aware that you must buy the minimum subscription.

Under your watch-list is a section called "Details". It will give you the symbol and name of the stock along with the industry that it is in. You want to make sure that the industry it is in is in the top 50% of current growth industries. You don't want to buy a stock in an industry in the lower half because it is too out of favor and out of date to move quickly.

"Life is like riding a bicycle. To keep your balance, you must keep moving."

- Albert Einstein.

Remember, we are looking for movement. In order to find movement there is an application for Smart phones called Screener. It may be free or have a low cost as well, either way it's helpful. They have a section called "Top Gainer NASDAQ". Go to the Top Gainer and there you will see The Top Gainer by percentage of the day. on the left side it will have the symbol and the name of the company. It will also tell you the close of that day and how much it went up in percentage. It will show you the open, the high of the day, the low of the day and the close. It will also tell you the volume it traded that day, we're looking for stocks that have sufficient volume to trade. The way I go through this list is: I start from the bottom, the lowest percentage gainer to the top highest percentage gainer. I only concentrate on stocks that are $8 and below. Once you click on the symbol you will get a page that shows you the chart of the stock. The first thing it says is indicator number 1. Change that to William's Percentage R. The second indicator is: Commodity Channel index and the next indicator is chart type, You want to change that to candlestick. The last is date range. You want to change that to 2 months. Under this you will see the chart they give you. We are looking at the chart for the smooth moving average 5, which is automatic, and we want it to cross the smooth moving average 20. We want to choose a stock that has recently crossed at the 5 and 20 SMA and has a good candlestick. **A bonus will be a pattern of a green candlestick followed by a DOJI, also, look under the chart and look at company profile, read a little about the company to make sure it's in a growth industry. Also, check where it says "news" you'll see the reason for the stock movement.** Thus in conclusion we're looking for the William's Percent R to be in the top range, the CCI to be in the top range, the 5 and 20 who have recently crossed, the candlestick to be good and the volume to be good. The reason we are choosing candidates from the lower percent gainers first is because they have not had a good movement that day and may have a good movement the next day. If we choose from the top percentage gainers it may have already gone up 40% and may have some profit taking the next day. This list should take you a short period every night to go through and you put these candidates on your watch list. If they open the next day with a good candlestick, 21 minute chart, then you can get in. WATCH OUT FOR PROFIT TRADING IN THE SECOND DAY BEFORE IT MAKES ITS NEXT MOVE.

Under the chart they have the company profile, which tells you what the company does and what industry is it in. It also includes basic information and news. It is important to look at the news so that you see the reason why the stock is moving.

Keep in mind the law of physics: *what is in motion will stay in motion.*

Under "Details", on the right side of the chart under the watchlist, at the bottom, there is a section called "Headlines". This will have interesting information about the stock you are buying. Thus, if you scroll through the headlines quickly you can see the kind of stock and interesting comments about the management. For me, I only look at the latest piece of news because I feel that is the most important.

This may reinforce or negate your decision about choosing the stock. If you are looking for a way to choose between two stocks that have similar characteristics. You can choose an indicator called relative strength, which on the Trading View platform and all other platforms it usually appears as the number 14. I suggest you change it to the number 2 and on the indicator you will see a number. If you compare this number to another, the one that has the highest relative number in a good industry is the stock I would choose, because it basically means one stock is stronger relative to another on a daily basis. Thus, you can put on your chart the relative strength index all the time or just put it on when you are choosing between stocks, whatever is easier for you.

I personally leave it on the charts all the time but that's a personal decision. In brief, we are trying to choose the strongest stocks in the strongest groups with the correct indicators. It's also important to pay attention to the volume, we always want the volume to be more than the average daily volume of the stock. The screener app is not good for this if you want to check average daily volume Yahoo is good for that.

Trading View will also allow you to publish ideas and allow you to take snapshots of certain charts and exchange ideas. We also encourage an exchange of ideas in our chat room on our website penniestothousands.com. In fact, when you are in our chat room you should put the symbol and then if it is an A+ or an A stock on your watch-list and some details about it, specially volume. Remember post responsible comments and only post things that pertain to training our system, let's keep an active chat room. ACCEPT CHANGE AS PART OF THE MARKET. THE MORE YOU CAN ADAPT THE EASIER YOUR TRADING WILL BE. For example, when you look at indicators like the William Percent R it may not be in the upper band yet but it's close and it's going in that direction.

All companies at some point may have been low price stocks. Over the course of my career, starting in the late 1970's, I have found secrets to picking low price stocks.

The secret to finding low price stocks is to find stocks that are moving on the over the counter market and look for our magic indicators of the top 20% of William's Percent R. The top 20% of CCI and the fast MACD has crossed, plus, the price is above the 50 day moving average. It is also above the cloud and we have a positive Candlestick from our Candlestick chapter.

I also like to choose an indicator on my platform called "The Price Volume Trend" (PVT). I want to see a number line that goes sideways for awhile and then goes up hard and strong. It looks like a hockey stick, long and goes to the right.

Once you understand the low price game it is possible to make profits but the odds are against you because there are manipulators and scammers. Sometimes people say that investing in low price stocks is like going to Las Vegas. Most people that go to Las Vegas try to win money but most of them end up losing. They do not build these fancy casinos on peoples winnings. They might give you some free drinks and some free food but most people lose money. In fact, the longer you play, the better the chance you're going to lose, because the longer you play the longer the odds are against you.

There are reasons why people lose in Las Vegas. THE ODDS ARE AGAINST YOU.

Why would you continually bet on something when the odds are against you? That's what a gambler does. Trading is not like gambling. We are looking for an edge, for specific patterns and indicators that have a high probability of winning. My indicators are not always right but if they are 70% right I consider it a rule. You will have losses but you cut your losses quickly. I like to look for stocks that have a potential to double or triple. BUYING STOCKS ARE NOT LIKE BUYING LOTTERY TICKETS-TRADE A PROVEN SYSTEM. ALL TRADING INVOLVES LOSSES BUT YOU NEED TO PUT THE ODDS IN YOUR FAVOR.

Below are some general rules that I have for investing in low stocks.

Number 1: Ignore stocks that are being pushed in emails or on social media websites. It is better for you to do your own technical research.

Number 2: Disregard tips from friends or relatives. These people are not professionals.

Number 3: Ignore stocks that people are receiving compensation for pushing up.

Number 4: Never follow free stock reports. If it's a free report it's probably because they are being paid or compensated to promote the stock.

Number 5: Sell rapidly, always have a stop loss sell order to sell your low price stocks. At some price that you feel fair, when it hits your sale order, you will be out. Never average down. That means when you buy a stock and the price drops, you buy more shares by averaging down your average price. Remember that you should have your stop loss of the amount you are willing to lose on that trade or the 8 EMA goal line.

Number 6: Beware when a company announces a reversed split. It is letting the world know they are in trouble. THIS IS USUALLY THE KISS OF DEATH.

Number 7: Always know your exit on the down side, use mental stops. A good way to sell a stock is to sell 50% at your first target level and let the other 50% ride until there is better news in the future.

Number 9: Do not take large positions, never trade more than 5% of a stocks daily trading volume. For example: If a stock is trading two hundred thousand shares a day, never buy more than ten thousand and buy it in positions, maybe five at a time.

Number 10: Don't marry a low price stock, they might have Let the chart tell you what to do.

Number 11: Always place a limit when buying low price stocks, never buy a low price stock at the market price. Always place your order first and wait to see if you get executed. Then try going between the bids and the ask. If not, buy it at the ask price.

Number 12: Remember, when you're buying a low price stock think of yourself as a pilot before you take off with your trade. You must have a checklist that you should go over. For example, here is a checklist divided in three parts: The daily part, the weekly part, and the 21 minute part.

The first part is the daily checklist. You must say yes to all of the following criteria:

a. Go to a daily chart first, that means daily chart action. First thing you look at is William's Percent R. Is it in the top 20% or close? If it is, mark a yes in your checklist.
b. Look at the CCI. Is it in the upper band or close? If it is, mark yes on your checklist.
c. Look at your MACD fast and did the signals cross? If yes then go to the next item.
d. Price volume trend: Has the price volume trend began to move up on the right side of the chart?
e. Make sure the volume on that daily chart is above the volume of the average trading volume of that stock.

If you answered yes to all the criteria above, then you can go up to the daily chart. Here is your checklist for the top of the chart:

— Is it above the cloud?
— Is the 5 and 20 day smoothing average crossed?
— Is the Candlestick positive?
— Is it above the 50-day moving average?

If the answers of all these questions are yes, we go to the weekly chart. On the weekly chart you just have to check for one thing: Is it above the cloud? If it's not, use the cloud point on the weekly chart as your 50% exit point. Remember, the thicker the cloud, the tougher the resistance.

Next thing you need to look at, is the 21 minute chart. The reason we are looking at this, is because 21 is a Fibonacci number and 21 minutes is enough time to see if that stock is going to be positive for that day. On most free trading platforms, the 21 minute chart is a paid option.

When we are setting trading goals many of you are scared to set a big goal. All goals should be SMART.

Specific, even if you have a large goal for the future, break it down into small goals (monthly).

Measurable, make sure you can measure your progress, short or long term.

Attainable, in your goals you have to believe you can reach it even if you have much larger goals. Break them down into small goals. For example, if you are on a football field and you have 100 yards to go with a touchdown being your ultimate goal, you may need to break it down in a series of smaller goals, like 10 yards at a time.

Relevant, make sure your goals are relevant to your values. For example, if your goal is to meditate on top of a mountain in Nepal, you may not want to say, "I want to drive a red Ferrari."

Time table, you must have a definitive time table for obtaining your goals. Some may take one week, others a month or years. The goal must have a time table of achievement. NEW RESEARCH IN THIS AREA SAYS YOU MAY REPLACE IT WITH THE BEST POSSIBLE TIME. The reason for this is because sometimes it may take more or less time for your best possible goal to reach you.

I know your life isn't perfect but be grateful for the special moments that make it special now. I know that starting something new or starting it over can be scary and overwhelming. But what most people don't realize is that our human mind is designed to change and adapt.

A course at Harvard teaches you about positive MINDSET and one of the tricks or exercises they have you do is to pretend like you are going in a time machine and you meet yourself in the future. You ask yourself questions like, "Of all my years of trading, what rules did I learn the best?" "What can I do different if I started trading over again?"

I know change is not always easy, especially if you have the responsibility of supporting a family, extended family or have a certain difficult situation. But don't let your age or current situation hold you back. If you're feeling negative about anything remember to DEC your negatives with a positive affirmation, visualizations with details, and anchor it with something physical.

We settle for less, it is drilled into us that we can't fail anything. Please be aware that in trading, there will be days when you will fail. Losses are an inevitable part of our business but we have to learn to lose small, allow small set backs, small detours on your journey to your big goals. It is okay to fail when you trade but your trading losses need to be small and you must learn from all mistakes. That is why you need to have a trading journal to learn from your mistakes. All mistakes need to be learned experiences and all mistakes should be small. PAY ATTENTION TO YOUR NEW AFFIRMATIONS AFTER LOSING DAYS.

One of the ways to exhilarate the speed of your success is to do your affirmations in the goal state, the self hypnosis state, or alpha state. You may have seen old Hollywood movies to make you belief that hypnotists have special powers but they only have the ability to help you reach a deep state of relaxation and deliver the positive message and visualization to your inner mind. So, in reality, all hypnosis is self – hypnosis means you're the one doing the work and changing the thought patterns.

You may have heard that hypnosis is only for weak minded people but this is COMPLETELY WRONG! It is actually best to be used by all people who are goal oriented and use visualization with details. You are guiding yourself to make better your imagination and get stronger results. In fact, there was an article written in a major psychology magazine that was titled, "The Power of Hypnosis." This article explains that with modern scientific research the process works as if you are more intelligent and you can concentrate and focus on yourself.

Some of you may think, *"Hypnosis goes against my religion."* Self-hypnosis is a branch of accepted psychology and has no connection to any religion whatsoever. There have been countless studies done by major medical schools that say the alpha state/the self hypnosis state is very effective when used with visualizations, goal settings and emotions

Steven Jobs, Albert Einstein, Ted Branson, all used the alpha state when meditating or affirming their goals.

Be unrealistic in your major goal and maybe have a bunch of stepping stones to get there to reach it. Create the life YOU want with this trading and visualize that end goal. Motivate yourself and take the small steps until you get to that large trading goal. Feel positive about your journey.

A great example would be as if your goal is to drive from New York to California. You will need to look at the map and figure out all the points between New York and California where you are going to rest, get gas, eat, etc. Those are minor goals to reach your final goal of getting to California. You need to visualize that in your mind to reach your end goal.

Never go at it alone. Use trader communities and communicate with other traders. Never do an impulsive trade, always going through your pilots checklist. Good traders always keep the big goal in their mind. They know there are going to be losses, setbacks, and detours. Good traders never accept clutter or disorganization.

Envision yourself in a trading zone with joy when you trade. Try to sense a state of flow.

You have to feel it to believe it, according to what you see, feel and think will influence your actions. This is how self-fulfilling prophecies are formed. People believe something, it inspires them and they get results. Manage your emotions and your mind and then manage your mind.

You may say to yourself: *That was strange. How did I choose that stock? How did I know to get there? How did I do this? How did this happen?.* The more practice you have the better ideas you will have, better stocks to choose from, and better set-ups. The solitary nature of trading in home, can be difficult to expose yourself to new ideas and ways of trading; that's another reason why I recommend you going our trading community, STOP TRADING ALONE. You will be inspired to trade more as you grow with the sense of confidence and that is how creation works. So learn to trust your inner compass with trading, learn to follow that trading intuition along with our magic indicators. When you go in your alpha state, relax and set your goal but wait for the guidance to come in.

How do you create this kind of traders zone and develop the bulletproof confidence that's required to reach your peak potential? It begins with the understanding of the unlimited nature of abundance. There is more than enough opportunities in the market if you believe there is. You're aware of how your beliefs affect your results. There is a scarcity mentality which causes people to play it safe, this people rarely get what they want. Traders that develop a belief that's consistent with their thoughts and hearts desires will become more abundant rapidly. Wealth creates opportunities to acquire more wealth, and happiness creates opportunities to be happier.

I wish you the best and I will give you a little hint about goals: when goals include another person they are more powerful. See yourself with your husband or your wife, children, significant partner or whoever is important to you. When the goal contains more than one person receiving the benefits it is much more powerful and if your emotions are strong your goals will be more powerful. TRY TO PICTURE THE OTHER PEOPLE INVOLVED PLAYFUL AND JOYFUL.

"Good things come to those who Believe, better things come to those who are patient and the best things come to those who don't give up"

- unknown

4

CANDLESTICK SIGNALS

CHARTS MAY BE DEAF AND DUMB BUT THEY COMMUNICATE PERFECTLY.

"The real key to making money in stocks is not to get scared out of them."

- Peter Lynch

Candlesticks are graphical representations of the price action of the market. A candlestick can represent any time or period. A person that trades will have software that provides the charts representing different time rates from one minute up to one month.

Candlestick charts are a visual way to view your stock platform. Candlestick signals were invented by the Japanese rice traders a long time ago. I'm going to show you the most important signals for me. I feel they are are eight of them.

I have highlighted what I feel are the most important candlestick patterns. Instead of putting an example after each one, I'm going to recommend you look for the example in life chart on www.

stockfetcher.com. On this site they have excellent examples of the different candlestick patterns on old and current charts, you simply press on the example of the candlestick chart and you will find a series of examples to help you understand; I find this as a more dynamic way of learning. Their website includes many other examples but the ones I'm going to mention here are the ones I feel are the most important.

The best signal that I have found is a **Doji. What is a Doji? It is a stock that opens up at one price and closes at the same price irregardless of the stock price moving of the day.** Doji, with a gap up the next day or a gap down, it's the best signal I have found. I call it the Turbo Charts Signal.

Remember, the Dojis are what opens and closes at the same level at different times. Dojis look like crosses: many different styles and shapes of crosses.

There are new calculations required to interpret candlestick charts. They are a simple visual aid representing price movements. The advantages of candlesticks are that they clearly denote the relationships between the opening and closing. Because Candlesticks play the relationship between open high–low and closing price, it can be used only when you can have closing prices.

The Doji consists of only one candle. The Japanese say it is a very important signal. It happens when the opening price and the closing price are the same. It looks like a horizontal line going over a vertical line. It means that the bulls and the bears are in a state of indecision, if it occurs after a stock has been going up near the top of the trend sell immediately. A Doji signal near the bottom of the trend is a signal that will probably be a reversal but it needs a Candlestick the next day to confirm the trend.

Dojis are very important if there is a series of Dojis (one, two, three days in a row). This is very important and means there is great indecision. NOTE DOJI ALWAYS MEAN SOME KIND OF INDECISION BETWEEN BULLS AND BEARS PAY ATTENTION TO WHAT HAPPENS THE NEXT DAY IN EARLY TRADING-

The next most important pattern is the ***bullish engulfing***. The engulfing pattern we have to consider is two candles and its form after the stock has been going down in a down trend. The way it begins is that it opens lower on a day but then reverses and closes higher than the previous days open, thus the white candle engulfs. The other days, black candles or maybe your charts show red and green. I'm talking about black and white here. The most important thing is on the second day where it starts lower and then goes higher completely in goes the body of the first days. Shadows and tails are not in consideration, but the body must engulf the previous day.

Another important pattern is the **Bearish engulfing pattern.** This pattern is the opposite of the bullish engulfing pattern. It's a major reversal signal and it is formed after stocks have been going up. What happens is it opens higher than the previous days and then closes lower than the previous days open. Thus, the black candle (in your charts it may be a different color) completely engulfs the previous days white candle. Engulfing means the body of the candle completely engulfs the other day's candle, not including the tails (only the body). The body of the candle must completely engulf the previous days body of the candle.

The next indicator is called the ***shooting*** **star**. It is only comprised of one candle and it works because it is found at the top of an up trend. In other words, the candle going up and the **upper shadow needs to be at least two times the size of the body so you have a big tail** (a big thing sticking out of a small body). The upper shadow has to be at least two times the length of the tail. It should look like a shooting star falling from the sky with his tail behind it. It is very important at the top of an uptrend.

The hammer. It consists of only one candle. You can easily identify the hammer because it looks just like one: **with a small head and a long body which holds the hammer. So the shadow, or the part that is not the hammer, has to be at least two times greater than the body of the head of it.** This is found at the bottom of a stock down trend and it shows that it keeps going down. But, at the end of that day the bull starts to step in. The color of the body is not important (it could be either black or white or red or green). But then, the next day must be followed by a positive day of trading, otherwise, the hammer signal is no good at the end of a down trend. **Please note**: you must have a positive day after a hammer to be positive.

The inverted hammer only takes one candle. You can easily tell it is present because **it consists of a small body with the shadow of a candle two times larger than the body. The body is at the bottom, NOT at the top**. It is also found at the bottom of a down trend and it shows evidence that the bulls started to step in but there was still selling going on even at the end of the day. That's why, at the end of the day, the color of the small body is not important.

The hanging man is also a candle signal. It can be easily noticed because the body is at the top with a shadow at least two times larger. At the bottom it looks like a hanging man from across. This is always found at the top of an uptrend. When stocks have been going up for a while, you may have noticed a hanging man. The Japanese named it like this because it looks like one. Always remember that the upper shadow (the small part of the body) **has to be at least two times the length of the body.**

The turbo signal. I believe this is the most powerful signal of them all. It works in uptrends and in downtrends. It is magnified in how important it is when it is near the top and the bottom. It is formed by two candles. The first candle opens and moves in direction of the current trend. The second candle opens at the same open of the previous day. An open gap heads in the opposite direction of the previous days' candle. The bodies of the candle are opposite colors, like black and white or red and green. This means that investors sentiments have changed dramatically. When you are looking at the Screener charts, pay attention to charts that have the turbo signal that are positive, they will turn out to be your better winners. The candles visualize to you that there has been a magnitude of change.

In conclusion, there are many candlesticks and combinations of patterns. The best indicator of candlesticks that I have found is a Doji below the 8 EMA goal line and the next day is a bullish candle with a gap up above the eight EMA of our turbo signal. This usually leads to big gains about 70% of the time. If you are a swing trader (A style of trading that attempts to capture gains in a stock within one to four days), your signal to get out of a good stock with this type of turbo signal is a negative candlestick close below the T-line on a daily chart. If you are a day trader, you might want to look at an hourly chart and if the eight EMA with a negative candlestick closes below the 8 EMA goal line get out. I recommend when you first start trading to be a swing trader for a while, not a day trader.

For the lowest risk and highest probability of success follow our successful blueprint of candlesticks and our magic indicators.

I have included the ones I believe are the most important. The most important are these major signals that will combine with other Magic Indicators in the next chapters. We are going to talk about:

- William's Percent R
- Clear channel index
- Price volume trend
- Relative strength index
- Five and twenty-one day moving average crossing
- Crossing and above the 50 day moving average
- The PVT (price value and trend line) looks like a hockey stick
- Above the S cloud
- Above the 8 day EMA goal line

Hint:

Try not to take new positions on days when the stock market opens down more than 1%, you can measure that by using two ETF'S. First one: SPY. Second one: IWM. One measures the 500 largest stocks and the other a much broader base of stocks.

Thank you for your patience! Keep reading, you are getting close to unlocking the secrets of earning good profits on your trading style.

"You don't always have to know exactly what you do or where you're going. You just have to be willing to take the next step."

5

MAGIC INDICATORS

THE BEST FORMULAS TO
MAKE A PERFECT CAKE.

"Your investors edge is not something you get from Wall Street experts"

-Peter Lynch

What you are looking for with the indicators is to narrow down to the least amount of indicators and the most efficient way to optimize performance.

You need to use the minimal amount of indicators so that you can tell the difference between a trend and a noise. There is a lot of noise that happens in the market.

I am going to talk about **strules**. A strule is simply a STUPID trading rule that doesn't apply to today's market. For example: William's Percent R. In the old way of trading you would only look at that indicator of the stock to see if it was overbought or oversold.

Now we are going to use that indicator in a new way to pick stocks that are starting a large profit trend.

Whatever trading platform you use they will have free indicators on your stock chart. We are looking to find, maintain and edge that trading as a battlefield. The edge goes to those who can recognize and adapt to market changes as they occur. Independent investors have to apply the changes rapidly; the market does changes rapidly and that is why you need to have a good trading community exchanging ideas. For example, use the Think or Swim platform that you can get for free and trade a paper account of a $100,000. I recommend you paper trade before you start trading real money. THE REASON IS YOU CAN BE MORE PLAYFUL.

Let's say, for example, all the indicators line up but one. It is very close. You might want to give that stock a great selection but all the indicators didn't line up. You might want to give that an A+, thus, in the final selection you might want to choose an A+ over an A.

IN THIS SECTION, WE WILL REFER TO THE CLOUD AS AN ICHIMOKU CLOUD. THE CLOUD HAS MANY LINES AND PARTS WE ARE ONLY INTERESTED IN THE MOST PROMINENT FEATURE. WHICH IS THE DARKER SHADER PART. IT ACTS LIKE JUST WHAT IT IS FLOOR OR CEILING ON STOCK PRICES. WE LIKE TO CHOOSE STOCKS ABOVE THEIR DAILY CLOUD AND WITH SOME ROOM TO RUN ON A WEEKLY CLOUD.

When allocating money in your trading system, NEVER allocate all the money in one trading day. The reason for that is the market could have an extremely bad day of news and you don't want to get caught in the down draft of a strong day down in the market. That is why you want to allocate your money over a series of days to avoid getting trapped in this.

Be careful of the mentor you choose for trading is far more important than the strategy.

Optional 1 indicator that is used regularly is The Relative Strength Index. This is a technical-momental indicator that compares the magnitude to recent gains. I personally don't use it in the traditional way to determine if a stock is overbought or oversold, but I do use it to compare the relative strength of my group of watch-list stocks.

The number I use in the Relative Strength indicator is 2. You are just comparing the relative strength of one stop to another over a 2-day period on a daily chart. The Relative Strength index oscillates between 0 and 100. You will look for the highest Relative Strength Number compared to the other stocks. When it has a high relative strength number along with Percentage R and other magic indicators are lined up, the stock is a growth industry that helps me choose the stocks in my portfolio of 13. Always remember to never buy all the stocks in one day.

If you are choosing candidates for selection with our magic indicators make sure the volume on the trading day you are choosing is at least one and a half times more than the average daily volume. All charting services will tell you the average trading volume. If you need a more simple way, Yahoo! Finance has it for all stocks, the reason is we want to see movement with more volume, giving us conviction of our candidate.

- - -

"Price is what you pay. Value is what you get."

- Warren Buffett.

I have found value under 8 dollars.

There are many different types of charts out there. If you are going to trade low-price stocks, one of our favorites is tradingview. com. If you are trading with paper money my favorite is Think or Swim. This will allow you to paper trade an account so that you can get your teeth into something before you start investing. It is recommended to use this site to learn to practice, even though real trading is more emotional. This will give you the practice you need to trade real money.

The first thing you need to do is stock selection. We recommend that you download a free application or low-cost application on both App Store or Play Store called, "Stock Screener." This lets you choose your stocks for selection of the daily top gainers of the NASDAQ. When you press on the top gainers it will give you the top performing stocks of the day, from highest percentage to lowest percentage. It will give us the high and low for the stock, the close and how much it gained for the day. Once you have clicked it on it will give you a stock chart, the top of the chart. You will need to changer Indicator #1 to William's Percent R. You an change Indicator #2 to commodity change index.

Under chart type, you will choose candlesticks. Under date range, you will choose two months. Then what will appear will be a chart in candlesticks with the bottom two indicators: Willliam's Percent R and CCI. The chart will also include the 5 and the 20 smooth moving averages. You are looking for a stock where the 5 and 20 has crossed: the William's Percent R is in the top 20% and the commodity channel index is in the top 20%. When it gets into this range the color of the indicator will turn red as it enters the top 20%. If this meets your criteria then you can add it to your selection list to add to your large trading platform or large stock platform.

VERY IMPORTANT: Only choose stocks where the 5 and 20 have crossed recently because if you choose stocks that crossed a while back you may be chasing the stock, meaning that the stock price has moved too far away from the buy point. Thus, if the stock market or that stock should turn negative your chances of losing are increased.

We are looking for a green candlestick (positive candlestick) in a 21 MINUTE CHART. Now, there are 4 others to look at as well. One of these is the daily chart. If you trade in shorter time frames, called swing trading, you will need to use a daily chart (swing trading means: if you are trading once a week to ten days it is better to use daily and enter in a MACD).

The second and third indicators are the William's Percent R and the Commodity Channel Index. In the William's Percent R you want to be in the upper level.

You are also going to look on the daily chart to see if the stock price is above the Ichimoku Cloud and above the 50 day moving average to look for a cross over for the two averages that will help you getting in on daily. The candlestick needs to be above the Ichimoku Cloud, which is actually on the upper part of the chart, the other will be below the cloud.

You will use these two indicators differently than the traditional-technical indicator textbooks use now. The traditional way that people have used Percentage R in the past is overbought or oversold but you are using it to indicate the start of a new trend will always begin when the Percentage R is overbought. Then, you can measure the intensity of the trend by the CCI. You want both indicators to be in the upper level and the MACD to be crossing. With the William's Percentage R, the MACD and the CCI on the chart you want the daily candlestick to be above the Cloud and the stock you want to sell should be below the cloud.

Also, you can put two different things on the chart, called smooth moving averages. Go to your platform and look for smooth moving averages. You put 50 in one and in the other put 200 day.

Why is that? They are not Fibonacci numbers and you might think, *"Mike, you like Fibonacci numbers why aren't you using them?"* That is because the 50 and 200-day all traders look at that on a daily chart, so you need to be aware of the 50 and 200 day. Even in an hourly chart you should be aware of it because that is where traders are looking at.

Here are some things to keep in mind in the following order:

- On a daily chart, the candlestick should be above the Ichimoku Cloud and the 50-day moving average.
- Then, go to commodity channel index and look if it is in the top 20% along with the William's Percent R.
- After that, go to price volume trend to see that the indicator looks like a hockey stick, meaning the right side of the indicator should slant upward.
- Finally, look at the MACD. Has it crossed on the daily? If so, good. Then, go to your 21 -minute chart when you are going to enter in the next day and make sure that the MACD has crossed, whether you are using a daily chart or a one-minute chart. Always remember to check the volume against the average daily volume.

This is a very simplified version of all the indicators. For example: there are many books on the Ichimoku cloud, on the William's Percent R and Clear Channel Index. As the author and many years of experience, I am trying to make it as simple as possible for you to understand. If you want to know more about the background of these indicators and who invented them, the internet has all that research for you. Remember, we are using the indicators different than what the traditional books say. All you need to know is:

1. Is it below or above the cloud?
2. Is it above the 50-day moving average?
3. Is it at the top 20-percent of the William's Percent R?
4. Is it above the commodity channel index?
5. Is the Price Volume Trend going up? If so, does it look like a hockey stick?
6. Is CCI in the top 20 percent? Can you see that in the chart?
7. Then, you are going to look for the candlestick:

If it is a positive candlestick: GET IN. If it is not a positive candlestick and it needs another one to confirm, then wait for ANOTHER 21 MINUTE CANDLE.. The dailies will tell you if it is a good candidate and then the hourly will tell you to whether get in.

Once you enter a trade you will use something called, "The Goal Line", also known as EMA 8 (EMA is the Exponential, Moving Average, different than the smooth moving average). What is the goal line? This is a secret line that shows if the stock closes below that line. If it is below this line I usually get out.

For the smooth moving averages the 50 and 200 and the 8 EMA, I use crosses in my charts. In other words, instead of a line I use crosses: always different colors for you to see the color patterns.

In this case I know the crosses and I like to use (the goal line for me, like in football) is the eight EMA to set up any of the indicators below your chart to put crosses on it. For example: In Traders View I go to the indicator above the chart. I go to inputs and I change it to

8 and then I go to the style and it will give me a color screen of the color choice I want to use for the 8 EMA. Then, to the right of that, I can choose what I want the indicator to look like: I can choose line, line with breaks, crosses... I choose crosses so I know that that's the area I want it not to violate. Also the intensity of the color in size is you can move the bullet target next to the color you choose for how large you want the crosses to be. It's the line that I use to help me stay in the stock.

I will like to make it an extra thick line and a color that represents the goal line for me. I will use whatever you want to use for the goal line that will keep you in. Remember, we have many indicators that have to line up to get into the stock. To stay into the stock all we need is a positive candlestick that closes above the 8 EMA goal line. If the stock price should get too extended above the goal line, the eight EMA, you might think of getting out because the Eight EMA acts like a rubber band. If it's too stretched to the upside it's going to come back to the eight EMA.

ALWAYS BE AWARE OF WERE THE CLOUD IS THE THICKER THE CLOUD IS BECOMING THE MORE POWERFUL IT IS. IT WILL SOMETIMES HELP YOU STAY IN A TRADE.

Sometimes during the day it will go below there and it will pop up. For you to sell the stock it must close below the goal line and be a negative Candlestick. Sometimes it will take you out of the stock but then it will turn around and go back above the goal line. When this happens and all your indicators are still positive, then you want to reenter the stock again. All you lose is a little price and commission to get back into the stock.

For example: we looked at the Percentage R and the CCI. They were at the top 20-percent so we want to keep looking at the stock. We look at the MACD and maybe it's time for us to get back in. It runs for a while (who knows for how many days). One day something happens and it closes below your goal line. The 8 EMA. You get up you have a profit you get out now it might come back like you said and also if the stock is trending up and you get a DOJI you might want to get out.

In most cases it might go down, but it might prevent you from getting a big loss. What is crucial is I'm not going to buy a stock if it's below the cloud. Never buy a stock if it's below the 50 day moving average. Also remember that one of the Magic Indicators I like is the Price Volume Trend (PVT), that's an indicator below the chart and we want it to look like a hockey stick: the sharper the angle, the stronger the stock.

ALWAYS KEEP A MAGNIFYING GLASS AT YOUR DESK TO HELP YOU READ YOUR CHARTS CAREFULLY.

I'm not going to buy a stock below the 50-smooth-moving average where the MACD hasn't crossed 21 minutes. I'm not going to buy a stock where I don't have Percentage R and CCI is in the top 20-percent band.

Whatever platform you use you can make up a new list of low price stocks; favorite stocks for you to look at everyday. Then, when you enter, you enter by looking at the 21 minutes. In other words, you want to see the daily indicators lining up. The day you are going to enter the stock you want to look at the 21-minute Candlestick Chart and make sure that it is positive because between the time you found the stock, the night before and the day you've entered you don't want any micro or macro news to affect your stock buy. You want to enter the stock with positive momental which you would get from the 21 minute positive candlestick. Always be aware of the volume on a daily basis.

This is really the lazy men's secret to low-price stocks because all you have to look for is the Percentage R, the top 20%, the CCI at the top and the Price Volume Trend. After that, you decide and turn around. *"Hey, on the 21 minute, do we have MACD? Are we have above the cloud? We're above 50 SMA so thus you can buy."*

LOOK FOR THE LOW PRICE LEADERS WITH GOOD RELATIVE STRENGTH.

Live the life you were destined to live.

I insist this technique will work for you. I don't want hope or luck to work for you. This is a scientific proving system along with positive statement goal center with DECing and cleaning the negative out of you. This is a successful way to enter a stock. If you've been trading and haven't had things go the way you want this system will work. It isn't your fault, your not alone. You've got to clear the negatives out and use the new system.

This combination of secret techniques that we're using are secret ingredients: the secret indicators when used properly. Always remember that. They are indicators and just like, when you make a pie or cake, you've got to have the right proportions and right things we're giving to you in this book. A couple are secret ingredients of eliminating your negative attitudes or negative beliefs and placing a mind that is positive and goal oriented, attracting to abundance in stock trading. I'm giving you the exact system that leads to ABUNDANCE that is the science of trading.

- - -

The secret of this system, once again, is you need to clean your subconscious energy: the negative off that, put it to a neutral state and tilt it to the positive. Bringing in positive, having your goal attracted to you and then give you the system, the edges, to trade the stock.

GOALS NEED TO BE CLEAR:

WHAT KIND OF EXPERIENCES DO I WANT TO HAVE?
HOW MUCH TIME DO I SPENT STUDYING MYSELF?
WHAT SORT OF THINGS DO I WANT TO LEARN?
WHAT IS MY IDEAL TRADING PATTERN?
DO I UPDATE MY THOUGHT PATTERNS?
WHAT NEW POSITIVE HABITS DO I WANT TO DEVELOP?
HOW MUCH DO I SPEND TIME WITH LIKE-MINDED PEOPLE
WHAT KIND OF BOOKS DO I READ?
WHAT DOES MY TRADING AREA LOOK LIKE?
DO I RECOGNIZE MY FELLOW TRADERS?
WHAT KIND OF AUDIO AND VIDEO DO I PAY ATTENTION TO?

With our community of support, our website PenniestoThousands. com, our Facebook page, and our trading community, you will all have ideas flowing to you as long as you act as the genius helping others: a real support community.

I know that many of you have been closed minded or frustrated before. You have had some winners but then a bunch of losers. Maybe you are confused of the money management, maybe you didn't use the right combination of indicators, maybe you didn't use the correct time zones of the Candlesticks, whatever but things are going to change now. I know many of you have used other systems and have felt disappointed and even bitter. The other systems didn't work but I don't call MYSELF a *guru*. That's why you don't need to hope for a miracle because I'm showing you the exact system that's as simple as cleaning your subconscious slate, replacing it with positive goal oriented trading state, anchoring it following our indicators, deciding what you want to trade, looking at the right charts, looking at the right time zone of the charts, using your money and risk management and letting the money flow.

You probably have struggled all your life. You have probably worked all your life but the blue print is here to change that subconscious, DEC that negative beliefs, thoughts, ideas, words or actions and replace them with positive goal oriented state of mind and then anchor it physically, you will absorb prosperity through my systems with trading low price stocks.

I know many of you have been skeptical and you've said: *"Oh that's crazy stuff, I don't need to do that. I just have to move on the chapters on indicators or the chapters on trading stocks and low price stocks."* You need it all and it's a package; it's a subconscious and conscious which is a whole learning brain method.

You have to program your subconscious which is 90% of your mind. Then, we have to put the right blue print in there so you can trade. Now, we have to let you enjoy this manifestations and systems you use by bringing you the prosperity and abundance you want in your life to make you happy.

Remember, once you clear all the negative I don't need you to be SUPER positive. BUT I DO NEED YOU TO FEEL JOY AND BLISS. I just need you neutral with a slight blend of your compass to positive. Like I said, not super positive but that helps. You need it and you are going to the systems work for you, you are going to get empowered. You are going to find out with a new rush of positive energy and excitement, you are going to notice it more and more. But we want to manage those emotions right, we want to watch for the killers of fear and greed; we want to let the money flow.

TAKE A MIND BREAK. REWARD YOURSELF FOR A GOOD TRADING DAY. IT WILL HELP YOU ENERGIZE FOR ANOTHER TRADING DAY.

The solutions: the people—our trading community—are going to help you along with the book. With every good management system and good trade you make learn to cut your losses quickly and being able to make money, pull some of the table and let others run. You're going to see that source of power trading run through you.

People will want to know: your friends, your relatives. You tell them you've got the system now. You have a way or tool to get your dream life. Keep giving us all the feedback, all the positive trading events. Share with them, in our trading community in Facebook. Tell us the solutions you've found. Tell them how things have changed, demonstrate how the magic indicators have worked and you'll be able to help others. I believe it is a mission to help others trade and it should be your mission to help the traders in the community. You will be the genius or the *guru* of this program.

The way you look at the Stock Screener is to look at the top of the screener, which is called, "the top gaining stocks" of the NASDAQ stocks. The stocks are listed from the largest gainer down to the smallest. It will give you the opening close prices, the high of the day, the last price and how much percentage gain for the day. The way I scan for these stocks is to look for stocks under $8 and to look for those that have enough volume traded so that I can trade the stocks. Then, I click on the stock and then a stock chart appears on the next page. There are four indicators that you can change. The first indicator is indicator 1: you want to change that to commodity channel index. Indicator 2: you want to change it to Williams Percent R. Indicator 3: is chart type you want to pick Candlestick and Indicator 4: date range; underneath the chart you can pick on company profile, which will tell you basic information about the company and also what the current news is. ALWAYS LOOK AT THE LIST FROM THE SMALLER GAINER TO THE LARGER. THIS IS BECAUSE IF YOU CHOOSE THE BIGGEST GAINER THEIR COULD BE PROFIT TAKING THE NEXT DAY.

You are going to look at the chart in the stock scanner first to see if the five-day smooth moving average has crossed the 20-smooth moving day average and you want to make sure that the 5 has crossed the 20 recently. Then, you want to make sure the candlestick of that day is. Finally, you want to look below and make sure the CCI and Williams Percent R are in the top 20-percent.

The next thing is to take the stock and put it in your platform and see if it is above the 50-day moving average and the Cloud. If it passes that test, there is one more test to look at: go back to your trading platform on a weekly basis and make sure the stock is above the cloud on a weekly basis. If the stock on a weekly basis is trading above the Cloud you can still buy it but you look at the Cloud as a resistance point, it might not get through the Cloud, specially if the cloud is thickening. Then, if it passes all these tests there is still one more test that it must pass before you can purchase a stock. The next day, when it is trading, you look at a 21-minute chart and if you have a positive 21-minute candle then you can buy the stock.

If you are not able to sit in front of a computer you can use the type of order we are going to talk in the next chapter, —which is "Buy Stop Order"— just make sure that the buy stop is above the current market price so that we make sure that the stock doesn't have any bad news or there is large bad economic news.

You can find a way to make yourself a pilot checklist to see how your stock is done. Get a blank sheet of paper. On the bottom to the left, put the symbol of the stock and the name of the stock. On the right side, put the target of the price you want to get in and the group. You want to check and see if that group is a growth group; a group that has the potential to be a double. On the bottom, you divide it into five groups, which is called, "the below the and above the chart indicators." Make a, "What we are worried about" below the chart and simply put a 'yes' or a 'no' or a 'y' and 'n'. When you check the 'y' give it one point; when you get an 'n' don't give it any points. Now for Percentage R, yes or no? Why a yes? Why a point?

For the MACD the same thing applies. Did it cross from the moving average convergence/divergence? If so, press a simple 'y'. Give it another point. CCI: same thing; Clear Channel Index (give it a point). Relative Strength Index, is it above 70? You might want to give it a point. PVT (Price Volume Trend), has the end of the right side beginning to angle up? The stronger the angle, the better. Then, above on the actual chart, is it above the cloud? Say 'yes' and give it a point. Is it above the 50-day moving average? Say 'yes' and give it a point. Has it crossed the 5 and 20 over the last 2 days? If it is, give it a point. Does it have a strong candlestick or a double set of candlesticks? Give it a point.

Five below and five above. What does that mean? You've got a potential of ten. What does a potential of ten mean on a daily chart? That means is a good candidate and it is a good time to buy yet but NO. We want to put that on our Trading View, see how it opens. A 21-minute good opening candle, that's when you get in. We pick our candidates, although our app is picking stocks that are the strongest. In reality, yesterday, they may have had good games (8, 10, or 15 percent).

What is going to happen sometimes at the first opening in the morning? There's going to be some profit taking. If there's profit take it, wait 'till that happens before you get in. As soon as you get a good strong 21-minute candlestick, get in and you're going to stay in as long as the trade is above the 8 EMA. The 8 EMA keeps you in or out but **let's have a couple cautions of this:**

If the stock price trades too —far above the 8 EMA— it will always act like a rubber band: it will come back. For that reason, you might want to wait or you might want to take profits quicker. But, if it follows the 8 EMA or it is pretty close to it, you might want to stay in and your sell signal will be a close, a candlestick close below the 8 EMA. Otherwise, the only thing, if it extends too far away from the 8 EMA line, you might not want to get in or you may want to take a profit that's the only other time.

Hint:

The 8 EMA goal line and the stock price will act like a stretched rubber band. The further the stock price is above the 8 EMA, the more likely the probability it will break or snapback to the 8 EMA goal line.

Your formula for getting in:

Your ten points coming up with your Buddha Trading Number is only a candidate to get in. The next day, trading determines to us when we get in. We must have positive momentum to get in. It might not just be breath-taking, it might just be taking it down again; it might be a one-day phenomenon. That's what we want to avoid. Remember bold statement/text, wait for a good 21-minute trade and be cautious of it's two extended from the Eight EMA. If the general stock market as determined buy the IWM is down more than 1%

at the opening you might want to wait for it to turn positive on a 21-minute chart before you get in.

TRADING CAN BE UNDERSTOOD IF YOUR ALWAYS LOOKING BACKWARDS, BUT LIVE TRADING IS LOOKING FORWARD.

- - -

Trading intuition is a very powerful thing. I'm not asking you to use your intuition to choose stocks alone. In fact, in my early career I only chose stocks with my left brain. With INSTITUTIONAL research, later on in my life when I was working with self improvement with the subconscious mind, I tried to choose stocks with my right brain alone.

Later on in my life, living far from Wall Street in another country, I came with this conclusion: you need to use both parts of your brain to trade well; you need the holistic approach, the right brain, the intuition, the DEC, the visualization, the affirmations and you need the left brain, the blueprint, the systems, the Magic Indicators, the charts, the candlesticks... That's why this book is a wholistic brain trading.

I like to speak like Einstein that said.

I speak to everyone in the same way. Whether he is a garbage man or a president of the university"

Hint:

Everyone has a goal for trading and they believe they will be happy when they reach their goal, in reality, everyone should have a goal that they are shooting for but what people don't understand is that you have to be happy NOW where you are. You have to find reasons to express your gratitude even if it's the smallest things in life, you need to practice gratitude and visualization, this will help you reach your ultimate goal faster. Always find time for the things that make you feel good about life in general or in trading, always look for events and thoughts that bring joy into your life.

One of the ways to keep affirming your success is to pay yourself first when trading, as you make profits put aside a small percentage depending on your needs and either reward yourself with something or putting it into another account. This concept of paying yourself first is a good concept even when you do your general financial planning. Always pay yourself first.

The reason I repeat my self is because the best way for ideas to enter to your mind is by repetition. Also, the first time an idea is introduced into your mind you tend to want to fight it or resist it but after you hear the same thing set in different ways it tends to pass your filters and go into your mind. In our social pages, like Facebook, you will see people saying the same things in a different way over and over. It helps you, the reader, to hear from different people in different ways.

I've always heard that trading is a left brain activity, a system of mathematical formulas and black boxes. In reality, pattern recognition, which is really done best by your subconscious mind, is really a talent-like intuition to develop because we trade in the segment of the market of low-price stocks. We have an edge because the institutions normally don't trade there because of the lack of volume and lack of research and analyst opinions, thus, this segment of the market you have the edge. Remember, you must always have an edge in trading.

In conclusion, if you use the Magic Indicators with the right stock selection and with proper money management which we will talk about in Chapter 7; you can trade with a higher degree of confidence.

Hint: Make sure you keep a piece of paper or your physical vision board or download your free application of Jack Campfield, "Vision Board". I actually look on my charts in one computer. I have a large screen to enlarge my charts and have two iPads next to my computer that are constantly showing me images of Jack Campfield's "Success Vision Boards". These boards have my goals, my end goals: means, goals and daily goals. This images are constantly flashing and affecting my mind and help me program my subconscious mind to bring me the results I want. Remember, the mind doesn't know the difference between reality and belief imagination; view the images and let your mind believe them.

Remember to invite as much fun and pleasant experiences when starting your trading day. It will be as little as walking your dog or cat, enjoying nature by taking a walk in the park or listening to your favorite show or music.

When you are creating your vision board, bring as many senses to the vision and the image that you can. Make this part of your morning ritual everyday like brushing your teeth. All successful traders also have an evening routine of going over their trading they and their trading journal and learning from their past mistakes. You are always learning and trying to get better, always evolving. In the morning, when you approach your work area, put on some calming instrumental alpha music, find a comfortable position, close your eyes and take a deep breath; feel your body relaxing from your forehead to your face, down to your feet. Bring into your mind five things that you're grateful for. Maybe something that happened this morning or yesterday: express gratitude for this things using as many senses as you can.

IF THE PLAN NOT QUITE WORKING MODIFY THE PLAN BUT NEVER YOUR TRADING GOALS.

Hint:

All people are looking for three things: Autonomy, which means the ability to decide and control your own course and behavior. Second, everyone has a need to feel competent, they need to achieve masters in something. Let's expect this mastery will be of trading under $8 stocks. The third thing is that people need to feel that they matter, that they have a sense of belonging and they are connected to other people. Trading can be lonely that's why I recommend you join our trading community and provide positive feedback to as many people as you can.

Then, in this state connect to the higher brilliant white light, DEC all your negatives and forgive any mistakes you've made yesterday on trading or in life. Next, visualize your trading day incorporating as may senses as possible. Set your daily intention for trading that day with as much joy, excitement and gratitude. Kind of bless your trading for that day, anticipate luck and energy, count from 1 to 3, open your eyes, get ready for trading, stimulate the energy by rubbing your hand 21 times, hard together, with the palms together and shake your wrist and hands in your sides and feel the energy in your trading day. Good luck in your new trading day!

6

TYPES OF ORDERS

"You have to keep your priorities straight if you plan to do well in stocks"

- Peter Lynch

The first order you know is a **market order.** This is an order given to a broker electronically or any platform you use to either buy or sell, whatever the market is trading at that moment.

The market order can be an entry into the market or an exit order out of the market. A market order means do it now, it's an order to buy or sell a stock at the best available price. Keep in mind that a market order guarantees execution but doesn't guarantee a particular prize.

Traders should consider using a market order only when their primarily concern is getting the trade done right now. Traders use trading orders when they are ready to make the commitment to enter or leave the market. To understand how market orders work, you must keep in mind that the stock has both a BID price and an offer price.

Typically, a trader buys a stock at the offer and sells at the BID. Understand you should never use a market order outside of normal trading hours because if a new story comes out after the market closes the reaction to the new story is going to affect the price you will receive. Also, outside of the normal working hours the trading volume is very light and you might not get a good execution.

In that type of situation, you should always use a limit order, a limit order is when you want a specific price for better; it guarantees a price but doesn't guarantee execution. For example: if you're buying a stock and you want a better prize than the current market price, then, you put a limit order in below the current market price. If you are selling and you want a higher price, you enter a limit order above the current market price. You want to use a limit order if the BID and ASK price are not close together and you want to guarantee a prize you will receive. If the market is moving fast or the BID and ASK prize are close together you want to use a market order. ALWAYS USE STOP LOSS ORDERS FOR THE AMOUNT YOU ARE WILLING TO LOSE.

The next most important order for this chapter, and everyone should know what this is, is: our **Sell Stop orders.**

These are essential to know because I call them "The Damage Control Order". These are placed to enter or exit the market as designed specific price. A sell stop order is often referred to as a stop loss order.

Let's say you own a stock and you want to limit your downside loss in a stock so you identify a specific price that will activate your order. If the stock price drops to that price, the stop order to sell is triggered and then you receive the next executed order. This differs from a buy stop order.

A buy stop order is used when you don't want a stock to get away from you. This is where you identify a specific price that will trigger a purchase of your stock. This type of order is used when you want to identify a point where you belief the stock price will go higher, for example: a stock closes at $2 and you want to buy the stock. If it opens higher the next morning, in that case, you may put in a buy stop order of, let's say, $2.05. If the stock trades up the next day to the $2.05 price, that will trigger your order and you will receive the next executed order.

The other question you ask about your orders is: what's my time frame? Is it day or good till cancelled order? An order can be specified either for that day only or good 'till cancelled which is usually about 60 days, not forever. All market orders are day orders. Limit and stop orders may be submitted for that day only or good until cancelled, so the bottom line when thinking about placing your orders is you've got to think about 3 questions:

1. Am I trying to buy or sell?
2. Which price do I want? The current price, the higher price or a lower price?
3. Do I want my order for today or good 'till cancelled?

7

MONEY MANAGEMENT

AND NOW (DRUM ROLL PLEASE)

"Big companies have small moves, small companies have big moves"

- Peter Lynch.

The idea of money management and turning a small amount of money into a large amount of money is to become disciplined.

Trading is risky so only use money that you can afford to lose. The reason I say that is because if you're always up tight and thinking about how you could lose the money and how it will affect you: you'll bring in negative mind set into your trading.

The purpose of this book is to change your mindset from negative to positive, attracting to you solutions of the problems and challenges of trading. You don't need a large amount of money to start trading, you could start with a small amount. This strategy can be used for retirement accounts like IRA (Individual Retirement Account), in fact, it is ideal because of the large gains you can earn by trading low-price stocks. The money will grow tax deferred and will grow faster.

The philosophy of "Pennies to Thousands" is to choose stocks under $8 that the big institutions are not paying attention to. Second, diversify over a number of stocks so that your risk in any of them is no more than 10%, for example: if you have $20,000 to invest you will put it over 10 stocks. When you get better in trading, you may have as little as 8 stocks. The style of trading is to cut your losses quickly and let your profits run after you take a 50% profit at your target price. A good example of a target price will be to look at your weekly charts and if the price of the chart is under an Ichimoku Cloud an the cloud is getting thicker then you put your exit order right before the weekly cloud. That means you will put the same dollar amount in every trade, example: if you have $8,000 and you're going to buy 8 stocks, you're going to put $1,000 in each stock. ALWAYS DIVERSIFY BY INDUSTRY TYPE. STOP LOSS ORDERS WILL KEEP YOUR LOSSES SMALL.

The stocks that where trying to choose in our systems are multi-bagger stocks. The definition of a multi-bagger stock is: a stock that every time it increases 100% it is a 1-bagger, thus, a 2-bagger stock will increase by 200%, a 3-bagger stock will increase by 300% and so on.

Also, you want to make sure that your concentration of stocks are not all in one industry, for example: you don't want more than 20% of your stocks in anyone's industry. What I mean is: you don't want anymore than 20% of your stocks in biotech industry, solar industry, etc. When we place an order we always want to have a limited downside and whenever our target prices meet on the upside we want to sell half and let the other half run until we get a proper sell signal.

Remember, our sell signal is the goal line, the 8 EMA on a daily chart when the sell signal candlestick closes below the line. Our upside 50% profit-taking may be a Fibonacci extension, the level it appears on a weekly or monthly chart or possibly a 200 day moving average on the daily or weekly chart.

This is a philosophy for the swing trader that can't stay in front of a computer screen all day and watch his stocks. But if you are a day trader, you use the same strategy with the 21-minute chart. REMEMBER ALWAYS USE STOP LOSS ORDES IF YOU ARE NOT NEAR A SCREEN.

The most important part of our systems is to find stocks that are moving and meet the checklist of all our Magic Indicators. Remember, think of trading stocks like physics a body in motion will stay in motion: a body at rest will stay at rest, that's why we choose stocks off the gainers list stocks that are moving. For example, on our daily chart all our checklists need to be met and when we are buying the 21 minute chart it needs to be met. At the same time, you put in your entry order to sell at your stock loss price. After you've done that, you put an order into sell half your position at your limit price and let the other half run.

> *"You can do anything if you have enthusiasm"*

> *-Henry Ford.*

If you are trading 1,000 shares a stock and it meets your limit price, you'll sell half and let the other half run until you get a confirm sell signal. A confirm sell signal is the Candlestick on a daily chart closing below the goal line. Remember, the same time you put your order into buy you're going to put in a stop loss order in of 8% and a sell limit order of 50% of your position at your target price or the price becomes too extended from the eight EMA line and you receive a sell candlestick.

Hint: Only choose candidates to buy that have enough daily trading volume. You should never own more than 10% of the average trading volume of any stock. Also, never have too many of your candidates in one industry. For example: You don't want to have all your choices on biotech.

> *"Accept and manage your failures. Do not be afraid to make mistakes. Most successful traders have gone through multiple failures. A great treasure of wisdom is hidden in every trading failure."*

> *- Dr. Michael Kluzinski*

Also, at the same time, on here you'll have a traders community of people offering ideas, philosophies and blueprints.

To conclude, the idea is to not lose money through proper stock selection but when you lose money you only want to lose a small amount, like 8%, of that particular position and when stocks are gaining in price and reach your first target level, take 50% out of the position and let the rest of the position run for a while.

With this type of management, you can even have more losing positions than winning positions but your trading account will have a net gain in dollars because you let your profits run.

Keep in mind that when you take a gain, take a small percentage and reward yourself. That will help your psychological state of mind and will keep you on a positive trader mind zone.

Remember, forget your money management strules and follow this. Also remember to take a piece of your trading profits and reinvest it into trading knowledge like traders music, traders psychological systems or anything else that you feel will help you.

In the future, we will have on our website a series of downloadable videos and audios to help you DEC your blocks and we will also have special scientific programmable music that you can play while you are preparing for trading or actually trading.

Good luck! Remember money management is an intricate part of our system. Don't ignore it.

> *"The more I see, the less I know for sure"*
>
> *- John Lennon.*

Hint:

In money management is important to reward yourself with something with joy when you make good gains. They can be smallest thing as possible but you want to link your profits with something of joy. *Joy is the key.*

> *"Rule No.1: Never lose money. Rule No.2: Never forget rule No.1."*
>
> *- Warren Buffett.*

8

PUTTING IT ALL TOGETHER

"If you aim at nothing, you will hit it every time"

- Zig Ziglar.

10 rules to be happy while trading

Rule 1: Give up on your need to be always right about trading. You are going to make mistakes. The key is to keep your mistakes tight and let profits run on the other side.

As a human being, you might feel the need to be in control; control the market, control the economy. The market is going to do what it is going to do, like reacting to all the events in the economy. You need to react to the market, not to let the market react to you. Don't try to control the market.

Rule 2: Give up on blame.

Rule 3: Give up your limiting beliefs. First of all, these beliefs come from your subconscious and you now have the DEC system to clear away those beliefs. Second, you are learning a new system of trading, a new system of managing your emotions, a new system of money management. You can create constant and consistent profits that lead up to some of the big gains.

Rule 4: Give up on complaining.

Rule 5: Give up on your ability to impress others. Who cares if you have the latest car, the latest house, etc? You use your PROFITS to buy the things you want, not the things that impress other people.

Rule 6: Give up your resistance to change. You always need to learn something, you always have room to change. You need to change your subconscious beliefs, your regular beliefs, the way you trade. Stop resisting change.

Rule 7: Give up on your fears. You need to control the DECing system by feeding positive visualizations and emotion.

Rule 8: Give up on any excuses that you come up with. **Start with what you have**. Things will happen.

Rule 9: Give up on the past. A lot of you are stuck in the past. Let it go and focus on the present moment and how to make the most out of it.

Rule 10: Give up on your past beliefs. Stop living your life to other people's expectations. You trade, you sit in front of a computer screen all day, you make money, and you take care of the people you love.

Do not let other people determine the future you want based on their assumptions of what you should be doing.

Hint: Be in the trader zone create a FIELD around your trading and your trading mind. In the zone, practice gratitude and joy for everything in your life. Be clear on your goals, trust your intuition. Feel good by giving and receiving compliments. Stay in this rhythm zone harmony when you trade. On our website we will have available mp3 audios to help you stay in this traders zone.

> *"Know what you own, and know why you own it"*

> *-Peter Lynch.*

Why join our trading community? Let me give you reasons why I think our community is different:

- We are focused on the best part of the market, this gives us an edge.
- All ideas are actionable, we teach you what to do, and we update weekly with the newest information.
- We want to see you increase your profits and be successful.

So join this powerful community of trading people where the gurus are you. HELP OTHERS FIND THE JOY YOU ARE FEELING WITH TRADING. SHARE YOUR IDEAS AND POSITIVE MINDSET.

The purpose of this book is a WHOLISTIC approach to trading with an edge. In summary the title of this book should be: "Don't Worry, Enjoy Trading Happily". It is very important to approach trading with a happy, relaxed state of mind. The first chapter, "Trading Psychology/Clearing your blocks," was intended to try to clear the right side of your brain, your subconscious mind, of all the negative ideas and thoughts you have about trading.

When using the DEC system it is helpful to play music that puts you in an alpha state. This helps the suggestion enter more rapidly into your subconscious mind. We do that by using the DEC system, which is writing down or putting in your computer your negative thoughts about trading and replacing that with a positive statement, positive emotion and physically anchoring.

There are only 3 ways that stocks are trending: they are either breaking out, trending or going sideways. Remember 50% of the time they are going sideways, 10% of the time they are breaking out and 40% of the time they are trending. You are looking for stocks that are breaking out and beginning to trend up.

You are trying to buy stocks breaking out and going with the upper trend. The thing to remember is that triple bagger stocks will break out, trend up, then will spend a lot of time going sideways consolidating and then make their next move up. Try to find stocks with momentum moving so that you can find stocks that are breaking out and trending up.

Hint: Finding stocks is a process. Big gainer stocks can be like climbing Mount Everest, you don't go straight to the top, you go up to a base camp, spent a little time and ADJUST to the thinner air before you ascend to your next locations. BIG GANER stocks act the same way, they will have a good move then some profit taking and then they will move sideways before they make their next move so keep this in mind when you are looking for a good price to enter.

Sometimes you want to hold stocks in a consolidating period that is moving sideways when revenues are increasing significantly and is in a high growth industry. Otherwise you want to be looking for stocks beginning to break out and beginning to trend up with good volume. Everyday there are new candidates to choose from, if you should happen to be taken out of a good stock because it violates the eight EMA goal line. You can get back into the same stock when the indicators line up again and are done consolidating and you get a good candlestick.

> *"Owning stocks is like having children -- don't get involved with more than you can handle."*
>
> *-Peter Lynch.*

There are some stocks that have had large gains that I may have gotten in and out of 2 or 3 times. There is nothing wrong with re-entering a stock once you are taken out. Once again, if everything lines up, get back in.

Positive statements are more powerful when you use any type of music to put you in the alpha state. Our website will have special music you can download for DECing affirmations and visualizations and trading. Remember, your positive statements are always done in the present tense as if the action is taking place in this very moment. You may use a positive statement like: I'm trading positive today, I love and enjoy it. I AM STATEMENTS ARE VERY POWERFUL.

When you are trading it is very important to have a happy frame of mind. Our website will have downloadable products in this area. Scientist have proven that if you trade in the alpha state you will produce better results. This state is more relaxing than the normal state.

You can say to yourself: All trading opportunities are showing up for me and I am earning a good trading profit today. These suggestions are more powerful when you play them with alpha music in the background. Something else you can say to yourself is: I am so happy and grateful that money from trading is coming to me. It is coming to me in everything increasing quantities through multiple stocks on a daily basis. AFFIRMATIONS ARE MORE POWERFUL WHEN FELT WITH JOY.

Always remember that your positive statements must be in the present tense. For example: I am a good trader. As you say this your subconscious understands your present reality and therefore works to make this reality true. It is important to replace "I want" statements to "I am."

When you say your goals, write a list of statements that help you feel gratitude. This will help to put you in a good frame of mind. An example gratitude list could be:

- I had a good cup of coffee today. PUT LITTLE LUXURY THINGS AROUND YOUR TRADING AREA LIKE A QUALITY PEN, GOURMET COFFEE, LEATHER BOUND TRADING JOURNAL THIS WILL HELP PRIME YOUR PROFIT PUMP.
- I enjoyed playing with my dog this morning.
- I had a good night's sleep.
- I am enjoying looking at the sunrise this morning.

I AM TAKING PLEASURE IN MY OWN SOLITUDE

There are many things to be grateful for. Write at least write 5 things during the day and at night.

You must believe that your trading goal is within your reach. If you are repeating your statement and you believe that you cannot obtain it you will hijack the process. So when you first start practicing this you should start with small believable goals. For example: I earn $400 a day trading a stock. As you achieve your goals your confidence in yourself and in the power of your positive statements will grow and this will allow you to bring larger and larger profits. The best way to implant a positive statement is to release your mind from all the desires of the statement. Say the positive statement to yourself as if it has already happened, something that is true and obvious.

Use repetition to reinforce the effects of the positive statements. Positive statements are extremely useful in causing fundamental change not only in behavior and beliefs but in all conditions of your trading life. When a positive statement is injected into your subconscious mind through repetition the effect is tremendous. This will take some practice and does not show itself overnight. Be patient as it is a gradual and accumulative process. REPETITION WITH JOY IS THE KEY.

While positive statements are good they are even more powerful when combined with positive visualization. This process involves visualizing the end result of your goal while you are giving yourself positive statements in a relaxed state of mind. For example, visualize that you just purchased a new car with trading profits from low price stocks. To help visualize, feel the sense of joy in owning the car. What type of car is it? What does the interior look like? What color is it? How fast are you driving the car? Who is in the car with you?

If you are not good in visualizing pretend that you are in a movie theater and in front of you on the big screen is you driving the car somewhere. See it in front of you, see the screen as large as it can be: it's the movie of your trading profits like.

Make the film as descriptive and detailed as possible. Try to see yourself in that car and look at the interior. Is it leather? What do the dials look like? Etc. Do not get stuck in the term visualization as different people have different senses. My dominating sense is the sense of touch. I need to feel things so in order to visualize myself in the car. So I would be visualizing myself feeling the leather, sensing the dials, etc.

To increase the impact of creating your visualization during the trading process make the image as realistic as possible, incorporate movement if needed. Going back to the car example see the car driving fast, see the colors and shapes, how do you feel when you drive it? Do you feel joy, happiness or a sense of fulfillment? A thought without emotions has no energy and no force behind it. ALLOW YOUR TRADING PROFITS IN YOUR ZONE.

The more senses you put into the video, the better it will be. Can you feel the wind blowing on your face as you drive the car? Imagine the smell of the leather of the new car. Can you feel the texture of the leather and the temperature of the car? The more senses you involve, the more real the image is to your subconscious mind. HAPPINESS AND JOY STRENGTHEN THE INNER MIND.

Here is another example: Picture yourself in front of your trading desk and your trading computer. *What color is the computer? What make and style is it?* See yourself trading stocks and try to imagine how you feel as you start to take profits and winning stocks. Feel the juices flowing through your body. Imagine the excitement that each profitable trade brings to the taste of your mouth. The trick is to make the image as real as possible by using all your senses and emotions. The more realistic the visualization process, the better and faster the results. CONCENTRATE ON THE JOY IN YOUR FEELINGS OF CHOOSING LARGE GAINER STOCKS.

How can you practice this technique?

You can combine your positive statements to create a more powerful effect as you're imagining your trading goal. Simply repeat your positive statement 3 to 5 times. Do not be discouraged if you do not get immediate results. We are all at different levels of trading development and some of us have years of negative programming and negative belief systems that we need to DEC out of us. Creative visualization is a powerful tool when done with our processes found in Pennies to Thousands. We can help you undo years of negative programming. Furthermore, once you get your first trading profit your belief system will strengthen and will allow you to manifest your next trading goal quicker. EMOTIONAL HIGH IS IMPORTANT.

Traders who regularly practice this find that this state of mind and visualization process comes automatically.

If you are skeptical of how powerful this system is, use this wholistic trading system with a paper trading account like AmeriTrade Think or Swim. They give you a $100,00 paper trading account. Remember that trading is a process. At first you will make mistakes but then by programming your mind and using our good system with magic indicators you will get better and better and will become the guru of the future.

Others will be asking you how you started in the beginning, like what negative thoughts did you have? How did you overcome them? How you can help them with their questions and become a good mentor to them? I have reflected from the different comments of my students on how they became believers and reached the goals of their life. They all have appreciated the whole brain trading system of the Pennies to Thousands method.

When you are choosing stocks to put in your platform you want to use stocks that are in the strongest groups, the top 40%. You want to avoid stocks from old industries because they do not have the potential to double or triple and there is always the risk that these stocks may be reorganizing and may not have enough cash to keep running the business and facing the possibility of declaring bankruptcy. In summary of this idea, you should always choose stocks from the strongest groups and the strongest industries.

There are many controversial ideas in this book like: clearing your negative thoughts, buying low price stocks that are in an overbought indicator, but I find that you've got to think outside of the box to beat Wall Street to find the big trends in stocks. I wish you the best! Good luck! HAVE FUN AND ENJOY.

Hint: Ask yourself what is your greatest joy in trading, share with others your good ideas and keep believing everything you need will come to you in a perfect time, in a perfect way. Open yourself to unfamiliar instincts be the energy you want to be. Practice gratitude and magnetizing money profits in your trader zone.

> *"I try to buy stocks in business that are so wonderful that an idiot can run them. Because sooner or later, one will."*
>
> *- Warren Buffett.*
>
> *"In this business, if you are good, you are right six times out of ten. You are never going to be right nine times out of ten."*
>
> *-Peter Lynch.*

One of my students reminded me that trading zone is like the quote of this movie:

> *"The force is an energy field created by all living things, it surrounds us, it penetrates us, it binds the galaxy together."*
>
> *- Obi-Wan Kenobi to Luke Skywalker.*

Appendix

Questions and answers for Dr. Mike:

1. What can you expect from this book?
   - I am giving you a blueprint. **Follow it.**

2. There are so many books on trading why did I write this book?
   - This book is distinct in that it deals with your trading mind, using both the right and left brain with thinking. This book will help you clear your beliefs and ideas to overcome your obstacles found in trading.

3. Why do you recommend low price stocks?
   - Low price stocks under $8 offer good price potential and an area of the market that the large institutional managers are not concentrating on. We must trade stocks that have enough trading value.

4. How much money do you need to use this system?
   - A good amount will be around $5,000, but if you have retirement accounts they will work for you as well.

5. What do I have to do if I have too many candidates to choose from that all have the same good indicators in the systems?
- One way that is helpful is called the Relative Strength Index. On most platforms it will have a 14 number. All you have to do is change it to 2 so when you look at a daily chart there is a relative strength index at the bottom. What is that telling us? It is telling us the stocks we choose relative to each other will have a number and that will appear at the bottom of your relative strength index. So, you may have two stocks you are trying to choose from but they both have the same good indicators and candlesticks. Simply go to the bottom of the page and whichever one has the highest relative strength compared to the other, the highest relative strength is the one you choose.

6. What is the philosophy behind this book that is different than all the others?
- Most books on this subject in the market deal with developing your left brain capabilities and logic systems to trade the market but in reality the market is a living, breathing organism that is changing all the time and you have to learn to develop your right brain capacity and your subconscious mind to deal with ever increasing variables in the market. That is the reason I give you the DEC system to clean your mind and your positive suggestions so that you can program it to receive and interpret the ever increasing stream of data. Then our book gives a precise system with an edge to beat the market. THIS BOOKS ALSO

HELPS DEVELOP THE TRADERS MINDSET
WHICH NEEDS TO BE JOYFUL AND POSITIVE.

7. How does DECing work and is it safe?

   - DECing is an advanced clearing method of old negative beliefs that have prohibited you from reaching your trading goals. All you need to do is find a quiet place, relax, and enter an alpha state to put the negative thoughts and beliefs you have about your life and trading. Delete, Erase and Clear them. When you do this, do it with special music that allows you to go into an alpha state.

8. Do I need any special experience to use the system of Pennies into Thousands?

   — Anybody can use the DECing system to clear their negative beliefs, to use positive affirmations and crystal clear visualizations along with the trading blueprint in this book. If you are a beginner, average or advanced you can use the ideas in this book. To help you use it you can open up a paper trading account with AmeriTrade.

9. Can I expect great results when using this system?

   — **That will depend on the size of your account, the frequency of your trading, and your experience level.** The percentage increases will come with proper money management no matter what your trading size is. BE CAREFUL WHAT YOU WISH FOR.

10. How fast can I start seeing results?

— The professional mind set of a trader is an evolution that happens over a period of time. In the beginning, you will see your equity curve rising and as you get better at it, it will increase. An equity curve is not a perfect straight line going from the left to the right, it's a severe jagged line going the same way. You will make mistakes. As you get better disciplined, good money management and a clear subconscious mind with proper goal management your percentage increases will rise. Trading is a risky business and you can lose all your money, so you have to trade with money that you can afford to lose. It may take as little as 3 to 5 minutes in the morning to do your DECing, as little as 3 to 5 minutes at night to do your affirmations and visualizations in the alpha state and as little as 8 minutes at night to do your scans and choose the right stocks that contain all the magic indicators. As little as 3 minutes in the morning to put your trading orders in.

11. What happens if there is a day that you are trying to do your positive visualizations and affirmations but you are very stressed because things have happened in your personal life?
— If a negative thought comes up just say, "Okay," and acknowledge it. If another thought comes up just say, "Next." You keep doing this over and over again, and gradually your thoughts will slow down and then finally stop and you can place them the positive affirmations and the visualizations. Never fight a

negative thought because it will just try to come out harder, acknowledge it and let it go for the next one to come. FEELING JOY IN TRADING IS THE KEY. IF YOU ARE SICK YOU SHOULD NOT TRADE.

12. What about fundamental analysis?
— Do not put much credence in fundamental analysis. I like to look for companies in a good growth industry and that have a good exhilaration of earnings. I do not like to choose companies that are growing their earnings by cost cuttings. I like to look for companies that are in new future industries.

13. Should I trade on days where I'm feeling difficult and my mind is embroiled on a serious situation?
— I would recommend you don't. KEEP YOUR TRADING ZONE POSITIVE PLAYFUL AND JOYFUL.

"If you do not study companies, you have the same success buying stocks as you do in a poker game if you bet without looking at your cards."

- Peter Lynch.

- - -

I wrote rules of trading to help you with your trading style. Everyone has a different style of trading, and like the frame of a house, a person needs a set of clues to frame his trading house.

Klu No.1

The market is always right.

Klu No.2

Only trade the best set ups, you only need a few good winners.

Klu No. 3

The best way to choose an under $8 stock is to use a daily chart and make sure all the indicators have lined up for you. When you want to enter the stock make sure that the first 21 minute candlestick is a positive bullish candlestick. Only look at three time frames. The daily (to choose), the weekly (to make sure it's above the cloud), and the 21 minute chart (to enter).

Klu No. 4

It is better to not make money than to lose it. There are many opportunities. Everyday there is a brand new list of high grow stocks that meet your criteria. If you do not buy the stock right do not chase it. Wait until you have better opportunities the next day. Everyday on Screener there is a new list of top gainers in the NASDAQ. Only choose stocks where the 5 smooth moving average has recently crossed the 20 moving average.

Klu No. 5

Never apologize for a profit. To be successful as a long term trader you need to cut your losses quickly and let your profits run. Some stocks in the under $8 high growth company have the possibility of end up doubling or tripling your profits.

Klu No. 6

Try to cut your losses quickly and let your profits run after you take one half off the table.

Klu No. 7

After you sell a position stock take the ticker off your screen but put it in your trade journal to look at it later. That way you can see if you were right and why. Keep good trading records. Your goal is to cut down on your mistakes. Your trade journal, which is a nightly recap of your trading, should include some brief explanations of why you got out of the stock so you can go back and compare what happened. Invest 8 minutes at the end of the day to do this.

Klu No. 8

Do not hope, act. Hope is a disease. You will always be looking for reasons to stay but the charts will show you the truth.

Be in a perfect trading state, like an athlete before a big game. REMEMBER YOUR TRADING ZONE PEACEFUL AND JOYFUL.

Klu No. 9

Never try to catch a falling knife. Wait for a stock to bottom and then make a second bottom like a W. What is a great buy at one price may be a better buy at a lower price.

Klu No. 10

A good rule is to look at the 50 day moving average, buy stocks above the 50 day, sell stocks below the 50 day moving average. The reason for this is that you do not want to trade against the trend.

Klu No. 11

Never go into a stock with an even bet. If you do not have an advantage you will lose most of the time. Always put the odds in your favor. Use your magic indicators.

Klu No. 12

Never trade if you are physically feeling bad, sick or just had emotional arguments with the people that are closest to you in your life. Remember, an athlete is in a state just like a trader should be. TRADER STATE SHOULD BE JOYFUL POSITIVE AND GRATEFUL.

Klu No. 13

When you make a successful trade take a small percentage of the profits and buy something tangible. That will make you feel good and want to reinvest the rest of the money. Many people have trading goals they believe that if they achieve them that will make them happy but in reality to create a mind set of happiness to trade with. You must have your big trading goals but you also must be happy with your life. You must trade on a framework of happiness and be stress free. Some good examples are to ask yourself: *Did you enjoy the beautiful sunrise this morning? Do you feel gratitude and happiness for the good breakfast you had this morning? Did you enjoy kissing or hugging your wife or child? Did you enjoy walking or petting your dog?* These things may seem small but you must make a list of them to feel an attitude of gratitude when you trade. SMALL JOYFUL THINGS ARE GREAT,

Klu No. 14

When you hit a hundred percent gain in any stock take your original capital off the table and let the rest run for a while.

Klu No. 15

Monitor inside buying. Do not pay attention when insiders sell because sometimes they may need money for personal uses. Always monitor if insiders are buying. The larger the better.

Klu No. 16

Micro-cap stocks always lead the way out of a bare market. That is why I like monitoring under $8 stocks.

Klu No. 17

High volume days in a stock with no news are bullish.

Klu No. 18

It always takes longer than you think for reaction to occur in a stock but you should feel confident if it has met all the indicators then you can hold for a while. Only choose stocks that are currently moving.

Klu No. 19

Use a stop loss of 8% or use the eight EMA goal line.

Klu No. 20

Always DEC your negatives before you start trading in the morning. DEC them all. PAINT YOUR DAY WITH YOUR THINKING. THINK OF WHAT YOUR GRATEFUL FOR. HOW CAN I BE HAPPIER AND MORE JOYFUL.

Klu No. 21

Contrarians arc correct at turning points in the market but wrong the rest of the time. Thus trend following systems will make you the most money. The trend is your friend.

Klu No. 22

You should learn basic Japanese candlestick patterns especially DOJI.

Klu No. 23

The basic law of physics says that a body in motion will stay in motion. That is why the candidates that you look at for stock selection is from the top gainers of the NASDAQ.

Klu No. 24

Have a monthly investment goal and work towards it. If you make over $400 a day trading, you make a $100,000 a year. Wherever you are starting in your trading you must be happy with yourself first.

Klu No. 25

Avoid stock promoters in low price stocks. They get paid to promote and pump up the stock and then dump it.

Klu No. 26

Document in a notebook your winning and losing trades. Document your mind set before trading and the reasons why you bought or sold. The more you document your trading the better you will become.

Klu No. 27

Play relaxing music or images while you are trading. Do not trade if you are sick, have a head cold, a toothache, fought with your wife or husband. Investors do not need to be in the market everyday. Remember that our website has special music that you can purchase and download. In the future we are developing a sophisticated music track to help you with your trading. THE MORE JOYFUL YOU ARE THE BETTER YOUR RESULTS.

Klu No. 28

The first priority in trading is to preserve your trading capital.

Klu No. 29

When you are trading low price stocks never put more than 10% of your trading capital on any position and never put more than 3 stocks in any similar industry.

Klu No. 30

Even though you have met all the requirements of your trading position and you might be tempted to put more money in. Always diversify.

Klu No. 31

Always be able to answer this question: why am I in this trade?

Klu No. 32

The two emotional factors that affect investors the most are: fear and greed. Pay attention to the first part of this book about DECing your negative beliefs and attitudes. REPLACE WITH POSITIVE AND JOY.

Klu No. 33

Do not chase trades. Do not go after a stock after it has moved a lot and if you cannot find good reasons. The same goes with selling.

Klu No. 34

Cut your losses short. The reason is you are trying to look for stocks that are moving in an up direction. You certainly do not want stocks moving in the other direction.

Klu No. 35

If an external event or announcement changes the reasons for you to be in a trade, look at the indicators and let that determine if you should sell it. Do not bring up your old trading **strules**.

*Strules: A strule is a stupid trading rule that does not apply to today's market.

Klu No. 36
Always have your stop set and do not change your mind when the market price gets near stop.

Klu No. 37
Never average down. It is possible to buy a stock in pieces. For example, if you want to buy 100,000 shares of a stock you can buy 500 shares at a time.

Klu No. 38
Analyze and know your profit targets, meaning know the support and resistance on your stock.

Klu No. 39
Sell half of your position in big percentage moves.

Klu No. 40
Watch the charts, not the news.

Klu No. 41
Trade the chart pattern and stay with your magic indicators.

Klu No. 42
The trend is your friend.
Moving averages like the 50 day and 200 days will act like a magnet to stocks.

Klu No. 43
Trading is a process that will get you to your end goals but you should enjoy the process of trading.

Klu No. 44

Trade the same size dollar amount on each trade.

"The natural-born investor is a myth."

- Peter Lynch.

Klu No. 45

If a trade does not work out write in your journal what you think you could have done different for the next time.

Klu No. 46

Stocks go down a lot faster than they go up.

Klu No. 47

Always improve your relationship with your family and friends even if you have not spoken for years. Strong relationships will lead to a strong traders mind. Your improvement is just the tip of the iceberg. Many other benefits will come. SHOW JOY AND HAPPINESS WITH THE PEOPLE CLOSEST TO YOU.

Klu No. 48

Keep your trading journal as detailed as possible.

Klu No. 49

Learn to speak in positive action words. Whether it be about your trading, life or your witness to a certain event. Keep the statements light, positive and active. REMEMBER YOUR JOYFUL AND POSITIVE EMOTIONS WILL LEAD.TO FASTER RESULTS.

Klu No. 50

Always find gratitude in all areas of your life.

"I am not afraid of death, I just do not want to be there when it happens."

- Woody Allen.

- - -

Did you know?

The biggest regret that people have on their deathbed is the things they didn't try, the journey they didn't take, the systems they didn't use, the relationships they didn't care for. Regret is a hard thing to live with. Pennies to Thousands gives you a system and a blueprint to reach the goals that are important to you and for the things that you want in life.   How many times in the past have you repeated negative statements to yourself like: *I'm not going to be a good trader. I may blowup the account.* I need to keep instructing you over and over again. You must delete the negatives and replace them with positive affirmations and visualizations. Remember when you put this stuff in writing it sends a message to your subconscious. THE MIND WILL ALWAYS DO WHAT IS MOST COMMON TO IT. MAKE JOY THAT PATH.

This system will work if you're trading $5,000 or $100,000. There are some billion dollar FUND MANAGERS guys that use affirmations and goal settings in the alpha state.

Maybe you know the people of Hollywood like: Samuel Jackson, Ben Affleck, even Ellen Degeneres uses these types of methods in their shows. So if it is good enough for them it should be good enough for you in your trading plan. Using the alpha state in a deep relaxing state, you fill your mind with positive affirmations and strong visualizations.

It will help you support the change you desire along with our trading blueprint to reach your trading goals. YOU SIMPLY NEED TO USE THE TECHNIQUES OF THIS BOOK. If you need help with any of this my website Penniestothousands.com you can download my mp3 recordings and listen to them in the comfort of your home with headphones as many times as you like. THE STRONGEST TRADER ARE NOT THE PEOPLE WHO WIN QUICK BUT THE PEOPLE WHO DO NOT GIVE UP WHEN THEY LOSE

THREE POINTS TO KEEP AWARE OF:

- WHAT IS THE FEDERAL RESERVE DOING WITH INTEREST RATES?
- THE STATE OF THE DOLLAR WEAKER OR STRONGER?
- GEOPOLITICAL TENSIONS

- - -

If things provide you with good experiences that enrich your life they are good, but trading just to have things or a collection of things equals nothing. Toys are just toys and whoever has more at death does not win. It is in the quality of your life not the quantity of things you own. This is a new revolutionary trading system, which takes away your negatives, amplifies your positives, crystalizes your visualizations and gives you a blueprint to reach your goals. It opens your mind to a whole new world of advanced trading power.

While you DEC and clear your negative beliefs you open the subconscious mind through the guiding imagery in the alpha state. That is why this system is so useful and learning to use the power of the mind to accomplish things that people thought were once impossible.

I'll tell what happened to those dreams, it's called LIFE. Maybe you have used trading systems before and failed or maybe you used a trading guru that didn't work for you.

Maybe you are accumulating negative thoughts to bad trading systems, bad health or something bad that happened to someone you love, a problem with your children or grandchildren. As you grow older you start to conform to the norms of society: you have to go to work everyday, you have to travel and fight the traffic to work, you have to listen to every whim of your boss, and you have to live in what people call the real world. You were told early to stop daydreaming and go to work and be realistic. You were made to walk the path of others. Maybe you tried the large stocks or some system and you got hurt by the big boys, the institutions, the high frequency traders. Just open your mind for a couple of minutes and open it to the ideas in this book. THE IDEAS IN THIS BOOK CAN HELP ALL AREAS OF YOUR LIFE.

You always have to trade with an edge. You do not need super computers, super algorithms, or super high frequency traders. Your edge is your subconscious mind, trading rules, your beliefs, your use of intuition, your trading indicators, that is your edge. Nothing in this book you have read is original.

Hint: There might be certain delays in achieving your trading goal but keep working towards it, eventually you will succeed because you are programing your subconscious mind to dominate trading in lower price stocks. FEEL THE BLISS OF ALL YOUR VICTORIES.

King Solomon said it about 3,500 years ago, "There's nothing new under the sun." What I have done different is that I have brought all these ideas together in one wholistic book with a blueprint and a recipe. YOU NEED TO GET PAST YOUR NEGATIVE GATEKEEPER.

You may say, *"I can bake a cake,"* but did you invent the ingredient cinnamon? NO! You just put the right ingredients in the right order, the right quantities with the right mixture. Thus when you bake the cake you just follow the recipe that someone else came up with. I have taken an ancient wisdom with modern scientific knowledge and I have mixed the ingredients in such a way that you can make a perfect cake, the cake of your life. SOMETIMES TRADING CAN BE PAINFUL. FIRST FEEL GOOD THEN LOOK FOR THE LEARNING POINT. REFRAME THE EXPERIENCE.

As you are reading the different chapters you may be seeing the same things set in a different way or in a different style but I am doing that because of the law of repetition. Your subconscious mind does not pay attention to the information unless you repeat it over and over again.

Whatever your circumstances are (I've heard them from all ages, all income groups, male or female) this book can be your second chance, the second chance to reprogram your mind and to use the blueprint of our trading program to reach your success. Many of you have heard of the phrase, "It is better to give than receive." The trading Buddha would like you to know that it is not true. You need to receive as well as to give. If you do not receive you cannot give. In our trading community we strongly believe in this. As you are receiving and you will give back to the trading community through ideas and through your friends and community. You must allow the receiving to come to you and you must give back with blessings.

- - -

Bonus:

The harsh realities of low price stocks:

You know the great sense of excitement you feel when you choose a stock under $8 that doubles or triples? Well, no group of stocks makes it easier than picking stocks under $8 and yet on the flip side of the coin they carry the greatest risk.

There are a lot of MISBELIEFS of low price stocks. For example: They say a $3 stock can only go down $3. Well a $50 stock can go down much further but in reality they both can go down 100%. Most new issues of companies come in the 20 to 30 dollar range so how does it get below $8?

That is why we use our magic indicators. TEST DRIVE MY INNER MIND PROGRAM YOUR GOING TO LOVE IT. ALL YOU NEED IS A COMPUTER AND INTERNET AND ACCESS TO YOUR INNER MIND.

My style of stock picking is technical but I do involve some fundamentals. I look for companies that are increasing their revenues and not just cost cutting measures. I also look for companies that have a small amount of analysts following the stock but are increasing their coverage. Thus low price stocks under $8 with all the right technical indicators and improving revenue are your best candidates to double or triple. COME IN TRADER ZONE FAST LANE.

Remember, half the time they go sideways they are decreasing, 10% of the time they are breaking out and 40% of the time they are trending. You are looking for stocks that are breaking out and trending. Good luck in choosing your double digit stock gains! EVERY TRADING CHALLENGE THAT COMES ALONG IS AN OPPORTUNITY TO LEARN AND GROW

This book has given you all the magic seeds to grow your strong trading tree. May these seeds constantly motivate you to grow strong branches of happiness in your tree. ***Keep Calm and Just Believe.***

STAY JOYFUL AND SMILING.STAY TUNED INTO YOUR TRADING TUNER.FINALLY GET THE LIFE YOU DESERVED

- - -

"The greatest gift you can give a trader is to have the highest expectations of their talents."

- Dr. Michael Kluzinski.

I will like to tell you a little story...

I once started a student seminar by holding a $100 bill up, I then asked *"Who would like it?",* all hands went up. I crumpled up the $100 bill and threw it on the dirty floor and asked again, same hands went up. I then stepped on it with my dirty shoes into the the floor. Now, it was dirty and crumpled. I asked again, all hands went up, I asked *"How come you still want it?"* ; everybody said it's still worth $100. Then I said to my students we have learned a valuable lesson.

Many times in our life we are dropped, crumpled and ground in the dirt by life, in trading we lose our zip. I'm going to show you and your trader zone to feel special again.

ACKNOWLEDGMENTS

First I will like to acknowledge my daughter Michelle. She is just 13 years old and she did the typing, co-creating and simplifying this book. Who I think, will have a future career in finance.

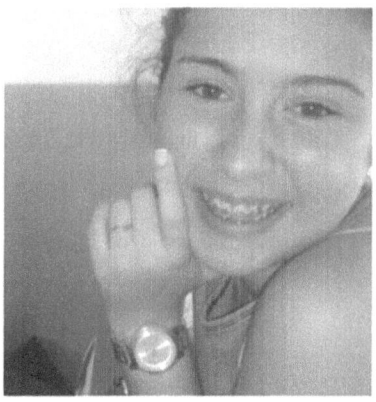

I would also like to acknowledge her best friend from her same grade, named Ivett Estrada, for helping me type and organize.

Also, to Michelle's teacher, Carmen Gaona, for helping me with the Grammar in this book.

I will also like to acknowledge Millie Lombardi and Michael Lombardi for supporting me in writing this book.

My lovely wife, Yeimy Muñoz, for helping me prepare and motivate me to continue with this book. She also gave me many alone time and preparation time to complete this book. I'm very grateful to have her in my life.

For my best private student, Bill Mathews of Orlando, who once called some of my ideas crazy and helped me turn them into Trading the Happy Buddha.

I would like to thank a man that passed away, Walter Sichort. He opened my mind to the power of the subconscious.

Another acknowledgement is an application I've used many times called The Success Vision Board. This application was created by JACK CANFIELD AND MOGUL WORKS. (I RECOMMEND VERY HIGHLY.)

The author of the Chicken Soup Books. I highly suggest to everyone that they download this app. Have you downloaded it yet? Are you using your photos? Do you have it on your trading area?

And lastly, but not least, my good friend, Frank Diamond, who always encouraged me to do my best in my financial career and was a great motivator in keeping me on track to finish this book.

www.ingramcontent.com/pod-product-compliance
Lightning Source LLC
Chambersburg PA
CBHW030748180526
45163CB00003B/941